REA

ALLEN COUNTY PUBLIC LIBRARY

3 1833 04

P9-AFR-612

Happy Sails

AUG 2 3 2004

AUG 2 3 2004

Happy Sails
The Carefree Cruiser's Handbook

Pam Kane

Reno, Nevada

Happy Sails: The Carefree Cruiser's Handbook

Beagle Bay Books,
a division of Beagle Bay, Inc.
Reno, Nevada
info@beaglebay.com
Visit our website at: http://www.beaglebay.com

Copyright©2004 by Pam Kane

All rights reserved. No part of this book may be reproduced or transmitted in any form or by any means, electronic or mechanical, including photocopying, recording, or by any informational storage and retrieval system, without permission in writing from the publisher, except for the inclusion of brief quotations in a review.

Book design: Robin P. Simonds
Editing: Jacqueline Church Simonds, Robert Spear

Library of Congress Cataloging-in-Publication Data

Kane, Pamela.
   Happy sails : the carefree cruiser's handbook / by Pam Kane.-- 1st ed.
      p. cm.
   Includes index.
    ISBN 0-9679591-8-7 (trade paperback : alk. paper)
   1. Ocean travel. 2. Cruise ships. I. Title.

G550.K35 2004
910'.2'02--dc22

                                                    2003018975

First Edition
Printed in the United States
11 10 09 08 07 06 05 04   1 2 3 4 5

DEDICATION

Phor the Phabulous Phloating Phlock of Phlamingos

CONTENTS

ACKNOWLEDGMENTS

The first person I must thank is my husband, Andy, who dragged me—kicking and screaming—to say nothing of pouting and offering a little creative cussing—onto a cruise ship so long ago. I was prepared to hate it. I didn't. And it changed my life.

Next, thanks to Jacqueline Church Simonds and Robin Simonds for sharing my love of the sea, my love of the written word (and the egregious pun) and for being publishers *non-pariel*.

There are not enough words to thank the Phlock of Phlamingos, with whom I've been fortunate enough to cruise both at sea and on land. They've been there for me in times of trouble and times of joy. Special thanks to the "other two twins" Pat Wood and John Mills.

I also must thank the campy writers' group that I've belonged to for almost twelve years now, dedicated to frogs, chocolate and solid writerly advice.

Writing is a rather solitary undertaking and the day comes when your writer's eyes glaze out at the words on the computer screen or printed page. Thanks to Al Rettig, Pat Wood, and my husband for "first reads." They kept me honest. I also thank Master Cruise Counselor Ernie Grossman for answering every strange question I had about the cruise business from a cruise travel agent's point of view.

To Bernadette Winkler, Teresa Lassek, and the incomparable Erin (Island Dog) for helping me to "put on the dog." To Barb Surges, who doesn't let chronic physical problems keep her off the ship and to Jim Heatherington for his professional insights on what takes place should the worst happen.

And, as always and forever, my everlasting thanks and love to my parents who told me, when I was a land-locked child in the Midwest and only dreaming of sailing the Seven Seas, that I could be or do anything I wanted.

3 1833 04683 7032

Happy Sails

INTRODUCTION

An almost-forgotten writer once wondered why this planet is called "Earth" when two-thirds of it is water and humans don't have gills? Maybe better, he argued, that the planet should be called "Ocean."

The number of cruise ships and those sailing on them tells the tale. We don't need gills. Over the past thirty years the industry has burgeoned to the point where an observer from another planet might wonder if there could be any more cruisers out there. There are, and the number of cruisers increases constantly.

How much has cruising grown? Thirty years ago when I lived in the Caribbean, one or two cruise ships called in at St. Thomas port two or three times a week. Today, ten ships in port on any day of the week might be considered slow. Fifteen years ago, ships ported in at Cozumel twice a week in the Winter season. Now, it's unusual to see less than three ships in port at any time of the year. Locals used to head for the proverbial hills on "cruise ship days" while merchants gleefully raised their prices. Now, every day is a cruise ship day, almost everywhere on the popular itineraries.

New ports are being opened and developed. In some cases, such as Calica in Yucatan and private islands owned or leased by cruise lines, ports are being invented to satisfy the cruising public. Very few port cities are unhappy as cruise passengers contribute more and more to the local economy.

Whether it's your first cruise or your fiftieth, you will wish you had "the book" on the ship, the itinerary, what to do once aboard and where to go ashore. No book can do that perfectly. The cruise experience is highly subjective, depending upon expectations, choices and individuality. Even in the same week, on the same ship, two cruisers could have—or think they had—vastly different experiences.

This book is the result of years of cruising around the world and years of talking to other cruisers on ships, on the Internet and in e-mail. It is, by nature, generic. That's why you will find words like often, generally, usually, sometimes and rarely.

You will also find the word "we" frequently. That's because all my cruise experiences have been shared with others. I've seen boatloads of things through their eyes as well as my own.

There's an underlying assumption in this book that *most* cruisers do travel as couples and that *most* cruisers do travel predictable itineraries, particularly in the Caribbean. Another underlying assumption is that the ladies do the packing for the couples. While these assumptions may not be entirely politically correct, they avoid tortured tautology.

Over the time since my first cruise book, *Cruise Control*, was published, I've been asked hundreds of questions about the cruise experience and done my best to answer. In the course of a position as an editor at an on-line service devoted to the cruise experience, I answered hundreds, if not thousands, more. In *Happy Sails*, I've attempted to answer the most common questions—and some rather uncommon ones—in the hope that there will be something of value for every cruiser, from the most nervous of newbies to the "old salts" who believe they've seen it all or, at least, most of it. I've also tried to put you, the reader, "in the same boat" with me—and give you a chuckle—with some stories accumulated from my time at sea.

Before you ask—yes, I was the one who packed her shoes the last night out and left the ship barefooted.

So, let's get that lifeboat drill over with and go cruising! Happy Sails!

CHAPTER ONE
BABY, LET ME TAKE YOU ON A SEA CRUISE. . . .
(Frankie Ford, 1959, Top 40 Hit)

In 1959, cruising was primarily the purview of the rich and famous. They weren't, however, cruising around the Caribbean with umbrella drinks in hand. They were "crossing." Those of us who are old enough remember newsreel footage of the great liners leaving New York and arriving in Southampton or LeHavre. There are still terrific old films floating around in boutique movie stores about romance and intrigue on those stately matrons of the waves.

Perhaps the most famous—certainly the fastest—ocean liner ever, the *S.S. United States*, was launched in 1952. It would have been difficult to imagine then, that it would be less than twenty years later, in 1969, when she hung up her flags for the last time. Why? Airplanes.

Today, cruise vacations are probably the best vacation value on land or sea and it seems like everyone's cruising. New ships are coming down the ways at a fast clip and prices are becoming within the reach of almost anyone with a credit card.

Where are people cruising? There's a hierarchy of cruise vacation destinations. Most people get their toes wet for the first time cruising the Caribbean, particularly in the Winter months, but it's a year 'round cruising hot spot. It's hotter in the summer.

There are three main Caribbean itineraries, the Eastern with St. Thomas as the anchor, the Western, which features the divers' heaven of Cozumel, and the Southern with Aruba as the big drawing card.

Some cruisers can never have enough Caribbean; others become more adventurous and branch out to new destinations. Lots of folks choose Alaska as their next destination. Others, particularly people on the East Coast, "do" Bermuda. Though the season is very short—only about six weeks—"leaf peeper" Fall Foliage cruises to New England and Canadian ports are a big draw, again with the East Coast crowd. Panama Canal transits are usually high on wish lists and are equally accessible from both coasts. Add to those the half-transits that bring you back to your departure port, eliminating a cross-country flight.

Then the fun begins. If there's a port, you can cruise there. If there isn't a port, you can get close. European itineraries, especially the Baltic and Mediterranean Seas, are extremely popular. The wildly adventurous—and those who can tolerate long airline flights—fling themselves off to places like Hawaii, Australia, New Zealand, the Pacific Rim, Fiji and Tahiti. Then there are the devoted collectors who will cruise to almost anywhere they've never been.

It's also true that the more you cruise, the more long cruises you'll choose. After a few cruises, seven days just isn't long enough. True aficionados salivate at the cruises offered in the Spring and Fall when ships reposition from one continent or location to another, offering many days at sea and great values.

Choosing your first cruise isn't much different from choosing your fiftieth. Several factors come into play and they are inextricably linked:

Where do you want to go?

Which ship would you like to sail?

When do you want to (or can) do it?

What will it cost?

There is no "one size fits all" answer. That's where a good travel agent comes in. You need to know what you want, then ask for help from a good travel professional, preferably a cruise-only agent who's a member of the Cruise Line International Association (CLIA).

Only you can provide the answers. Here are some of the basic, frequently asked questions to start you thinking.

What's the best cruise line?

There is no "best," it's which cruise line works best for you. This brings in the questions again: the itinerary, what you want from a ship and what you're willing to pay for the cruise experience.

There are, however, different levels of cruise lines. The mainstream cruise lines are those you see advertised on television. The luxury lines are, most likely, the province of your travel agent and your pocketbook. Look for luxury cruise lines' ads in upscale magazines targeted toward travel and the good life.

The more information you have, the wiser your decision will be. The Internet is a rich research tool; you can read flotillas of reviews of others' cruises. Just keep in mind people who are happy with their cruise experience are often far less verbal than those with complaints. Take the cruise lines' brochures with a grain of sea salt. You will *not* look like those models the moment you board the vessel.

How should I go about choosing an itinerary?

Most cruisers have at least a nascent idea of destination—floating about the Caribbean, whale-watching off Alaska, trudging through ancient European cities . . . and begin there. If you have a "must-see" or "must-do," make sure an itinerary provides the opportunity and the time in port. Some cruises are once-in-a-lifetime occasions. If you want to see Viegland Park, make sure your Baltic cruise ports in Oslo. Don't assume it will just because someone else's did.

Also, be aware of the number of hours scheduled in port. You may not be able to do everything you want to if hours are abbreviated.

Keep an open mind. As you read brochures, travel magazines and guidebooks, a stunning idea may come out of nowhere.

An experienced cruising friend says this: "We look at ports of call—and occasionally departure and arrival cities—as special introductory offers. In other words, part of what we're doing is evaluating them for possible return visits on land-based vacations." I think this is a valuable concept. Nobody in their right mind should ever think they could do Rome in a day, or Lisbon. You can't really even do Bermuda in the time you have on a cruise (although that's somewhat better). So the question becomes, "Is this a place I'd really like to get to know sometime down the road?" Using the cruise as a "highlights tour" with an eye to coming back really works, in the same way as taking the city tour first does. Buy guidebooks for the ports of call you'll be visiting.

Guidebooks? I thought the cruise lines did it all for you.

That's what they'd like you to think. The cruise excursion brochures are big on fluff and puff—and also big on price. With a good guidebook, you may be able to do shore excursions for much less money, leaving a few bucks for some serious shopping. The *Happy Sails* approach is to do as much research as possible before making a decision on shore-side activities. I also cruise the Internet using search engines to add to my knowledge base.

 Before a cruise that began in Hawaii, we decided to charter a sailboat for a day. Friends wanted to join us. I took on the responsibility of Cruise Director and clicked the keyboard. I found a charter boat owned and captained by a marine biologist and made all the arrangements in e-mail. We went out looking for dolphins and came across a family pod of whales. It was a lifetime experience as the whales frolicked around our sailboat for a couple of hours.

I see what look like some great deals on the Internet. Are they?

Most travel agents will meet Internet pricing or come very close. Shaving off twenty bucks won't look like such a bargain if problems arise and you're the one trying to solve them. There are very reputable travel agents who have Internet "offices." When you're doing your pricing, make sure you know what's included so you're making a solid comparison.

What services can I expect from a travel agent that I can't get directly from the cruise line?

It shouldn't be a matter of luck, but sometimes it seems that way. You should expect your travel agent to ask *you* questions, not the other way around, in order to find the best possible fit for you. You should not have to wait to be asked if you have particular needs or concerns.

As an example, a fifty-ish couple, with the kids finally out of the house, booked a cruise over the Thanksgiving holiday. There were hundreds and hundreds of children on the ship. This did not please them. Upon their return, they complained to their travel agent about the kid quotient. "Well, you didn't ask." Now, any travel agent worth his or her salt knows that Thanksgiving is the *most kid* sailing of the year. If the agent had listened to the couple, he or she might have had a faint glimmer that being around tons of children was *not* their reason for cruising.

As another example, a lady in her early sixties had been saving her cruise money for years. Then she heard a radio commercial about *her* trip of a lifetime and called the travel agent. Was the travel agent listening when the woman asked for a business class seat because she had leg problems? Apparently not. The poor woman stood—alone—outside too many of the itinerary's "high spots" because she simply couldn't negotiate stairs and difficult climbs. The agent also booked her for a follow-on trip to the Great Wall of China.

What's the best location for a cabin?

The top suites certainly have their charms and everyone should splurge, if only once. Just don't do it on a port-intensive cruise because the time for luxuriating is limited.

The old (and scientifically unassailable) wisdom says the smoothest ride is a cabin on a lower deck, amidships. However, with today's sophisticated stabilization systems, it's often tough to tell you're actually at sea.

Inside or outside? Balcony or no balcony?

If you are at all claustrophobic, you already know the answer: outside. People choose inside cabins primarily to save money, meaning they can cruise more often. Others choose them because they like to sleep in; it doesn't get much darker than within an inside cabin. This begs the question of just *who* would want to sleep in when interesting ports await?

Some people say that the cabin doesn't really matter, because you don't spend much time in it. The better the cabin, the more time you're likely to spend in it. Even though inside cabins are designed to seem as light and airy as possible, including extensive use of mirrors, they're still ocean-going caves.

Balconies are addictive. Once you've experienced sitting on your own balcony with morning coffee watching the waves go by, nothing less will do. Some of the charm is lost if you're early into a port and your side of the ship faces the pier. The view isn't waves, it's stevedores and the teeming hordes of people disembarking for shore adventures.

But don't just old people cruise?

Don't tell the honeymooners that! As cruise prices come down and more and more ports open up, the demographic goes down, down, down as far as age is concerned. Some cruise lines seem to cater to an older, more sedate crowd. Others have the reputation of attracting younger folk. The average cruiser is, probably, around fifty. That means for everyone who's seventy-five years old, there will be one who's twenty-five. And that doesn't count the kids who bring the average age down considerably.

 My husband and I did take one cruise that was definitely an "older crowd." We wanted the itinerary; it was beyond fabulous. Some of the ports were on the lifetime dream list. It was a two-week cruise, which rather eliminated people who could only get away from work for a week, so there were lots of retired types on board with us. Within forty-eight hours, the "Under Sixty Club" connected and, to our ever-lasting shame, the whole gang was busted by security for a late-night balcony party. The Captain was present and enjoying himself. He got busted, too.

As a rule, the longer and more expensive the cruise is, the older the cruisers will be. There are more and more short cruises—three or four days—which appeal to a younger crowd. The word on the waves has it that *nobody* sleeps on those. Until they get home.

What's the best time of year to cruise?

Any time. Some itineraries have limited seasons—but even within those, there are prime times. Bermuda can be quite hot in July and August, as is the Caribbean. The Mediterranean can get steamy in late Summer, too.

The earlier or later one cruises during the Alaska season, the more likely the temperature will be nippy. Hurricane Season is on the calendar as June 30 to November 30, but nobody has ever told the hurricanes that. Keep in mind the seasons in Australia and New Zealand are opposite those in the Northern Hemisphere.

Trans-Atlantic cruises, when ships come from summering in Europe to sailing the Caribbean in Winter, and vice-versa, are often a good value.

Holiday cruises tend to be prime time, as is the Spring Break time frame. Also, cruises that include a three-day weekend or other business holiday are popular with folks saving vacation days. The more prime the time, the more the cruise will probably cost.

What information should I be prepared to give my agent or the cruise line when I make my reservation?

Other than what you might expect—name, address, phone number, passport number and credit card number—any special requirements you may have, especially those which are health-related and any limitations you may have.

What are the pros and cons of first seating vs. second seating in the dining room?

We'll get there in more detail later in Chapter Eight, *Eat, Drink and Be Merry.* First seating appeals to those who live on an earlier schedule, late seating to those who prefer a bit of a rest. Further, on late seating, the waitstaff is less rushed.

How much should I expect to pay for a cruise?

Again, this is highly subjective and elective. In addition to your cruise fare, you may have airline travel or, if you drive to a port, parking. There's also the issue of transport to and from the pier.

If you decide to arrive at the port a day or two early or stay to visit the port city post-cruise, you will have hotel and meal expenses. Once on the ship, there is the expected "overhead" of tipping the wait-staff and cabin attendants. After that, it depends on how much you spend on bar services—soft or hard—spa services, contributions to the Gods of Chance in the casino, shore excursions and activities in port.

There are also plenty of opportunities to purchase high-priced logo goods, clothing, jewelry, candy and designer items in the ship's boutique mall as well as purchasing questionable "art" at the ubiquitous art auctions. Know what you are buying.

A high end for *elective* expenses is a *per diem* of a hundred dollars per person in addition to your cruise fare—not counting serious gambling or very pricey shopping—and a low end could be close to nothing except for the predictable tipping of approximately ten dollars per day, per person. Keep in mind that those logo goods, fancy costume jewelry, designer watches and "gold" by the inch will probably be on sale the last couple of nights of the cruise.

The bottom line is that the elective—and necessary—expenses may double the cost of your cruise.

Why would anyone pay extra money to stay in a hotel before or after a cruise?

Most experienced cruisers like the built-in security of being in the departure port city a day ahead of time. This is especially true for those who live in the frozen tundra and are cruising in the Winter. Snowstorms can play havoc with airline flights. One mechanical prob-

 Some port cities are just too interesting to skip. I talked a friend with whom I was cruising into spending three days in Barcelona, post-cruise. She didn't want to do it. Afterward, she wished we'd had longer. We always build in two or three days for London. Take advantage of the "there" that's there. Who knows when you'll return?

lem on a given airline can mess up flights throughout the system. Think of the expense as insurance against missing the boat.

What happens if my flight cancels or is late?

You will have to scramble to find another flight. Sometimes it's even necessary to meet the ship at its first port of call. If you've booked your air through the cruise line and the delay isn't a long one, sometimes the ship will wait for you.

What did we do before cell phones? On one cruise, the passenger complement was eagerly awaiting departure when the Captain bellowed from the bridge. It seemed there had been a massive accident on I-95 keeping people away from Port Everglades. They all must have had cell phones, because the ship waited for them.

Isn't it cheaper to book my own air travel?

Often, it is. The main exception is "open jaw" flights where you leave from one port city and end up in another. If you don't like the flight times or routing—cruise air travel arrangements are notorious for the worst scheduling possible—you can pay a deviation fee and choose your own flights. The cost per person for air deviation is approximately fifty dollars.

Keep in mind that just because the brochure says that you arrive at your debarkation port at 8:00 a.m., don't book a 10:00 a.m. flight.

Are single people welcome on cruises?

Cruise ships are not Noah's Ark. The "Unsinkable Molly Brown" certainly traveled as a single and, according to all reports, had a heck of a good time. More about this in Chapter Five.

Is a passport a requirement to cruise?

It's just plain silly *not* to have a passport. There are some countries—Canada, Mexico, and some Caribbean islands—which accept a raised seal birth certificate and a current, valid photo ID. However—and this is a big *however*—the world is a changed place since September 11, 2001. The only absolute proof of citizenship one can have is a passport.

Some people complain about the cost of a passport. They are good for ten years and amortize at less than ten dollars per year, including the cost of the photo and the postage to mail the application. They also offer the stunning opportunity to look even goofier, more sinister or lots worse than you do on your driver's license picture.

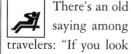 There's an old saying among travelers: "If you look worse than your passport photo, you really need a vacation."

I'm about to get married and we're cruising for our honeymoon. What do I do about changing my name?

You can't change your name until your name is changed unless you want to go through bizarre hassles. The most important thing is that your travel documents match the other identification you have. If your passport or other ID is in your maiden name, make sure your cruise ticket says "Susie Smith"—your old name—rather than "Susie Jones"—your new one. You might be able to skate on your cruise ticket, but make *totally* sure—in the wake of 9/11—that your airline tickets match your ID. Otherwise, your new husband might be enjoying the honeymoon alone.

Hold on. I don't *ever* intend to become "Susie Jones." What about that?

The one and only place where I believe it's essential to use your married name is on your passport. If you're in a Third-World country and either you or your spouse falls ill—or Heaven forbid, dies—you will need some proof that you are, in fact, married and you're able to order or approve medical care (or other sorts of care) for your partner. Apply for a new passport and use your maiden or professional name as your "middle" name so it will match your other identification papers.

If you are traveling with a partner or friend to whom you are *not* married, you should each carry a notarized permission statement (Limited Power of Attorney in legal-speak) to order medical care.

All my own identification, including a purse-full of credit cards and my driver's license are in the name you'll see on the cover of this book. My passport has "Kane" as the middle identifier and my husband's surname as my surname. Make sure, however, that your travel agent understands this.

Some countries only ask for a photo ID and a raised-seal birth certificate. What if I don't have the same last name as I did when I was born?

This confuses me, too. The best approach is to take along a copy of your marriage certificate. However, in the wake of 9/11 it is just plain felony-stupid not to have a passport.

I want to take my children on a special trip. I've heard horror stories of single parents or parents traveling *sans* spouse with kids having a hard time. What's up?

Airlines and cruise lines don't want to be responsible for a kidnaping. I ran into this situation myself as I stood at the airline check-in counter with my offspring. To be belt-and-suspenders careful, take along a notarized statement from the kids' other parent(s) that they're permitted to travel with you, especially if you're taking a kid's pal to keep him or her company. To be super careful, make sure flight numbers and identification of the ship are included in the document. As a practical matter, if you're taking a domestic airline to a U.S. port, you probably won't have any trouble.

Why do I need to provide an emergency phone number with my travel papers?

For emergencies. The most likely one is a ship arriving late at its destination port. The Purser's office gets on the phone and starts calling those emergency numbers. Unless you've made arrangements for hired transportation from the port, in which case it's up to the livery company to check your schedule, make sure the emergency number belongs to the person who's supposed to be picking you up, not somebody at the office—most cruises "turn" on weekend days.

Aren't at-sea days boring? Won't I get cabin fever looking at nothing but waves?

Not if the Cruise Director and staff can help it. They can keep you going almost from one sunrise to the next one. However, some people really like to look at waves. We'll talk more about this in Chapter Seven: *One Day at a Time.*

What if I just can't convince my spouse to go on a cruise?

If divorce is out of the question, cruise with a friend. When the spouse hears the stories and sees the photos, the next cruise should be a slam dunk. We'll talk more about this in Chapter Six: *This is Not Noah's Ark.*

I keep hearing about upgrades. What's the story?

There's the myth of the Upgrade Fairy. It's sort of like the Tooth Fairy. The most expensive and least expensive cabins tend to be sold out first. Often, a cruise line will upgrade an early booking to an upper-level cabin so they can sell more of the less expensive ones, filling up the ship. The secret is making sure that your upgrade really *is* an upgrade. A higher category cabin in a location underneath the disco might not be exactly pleasing. Always book a cabin that you will be happy with and don't wait around for the Upgrade Fairy.

If you are offered an upgrade, your best resource will be a deck plan of the ship. If you don't want to move, don't. This is where your travel agent can help.

I heard friends talking about getting their "travel documents." Do they mean passports or what?

No. Travel documents is the highbrow term used by the cruise industry to mean tickets.

What happens if I don't get my documents before I'm to leave?

Worrieth not. Get your booking number from your travel

agent when you make your final payment. Show up at the pier and someone will assist you. So long as you are on the manifest, you don't need those documents.

I was on deck just after our ship left port. A small boat pulled up beside us and someone got off the ship and into the boat. Did he change his mind about taking the cruise?

That's a little exercise that most people never observe because they're too busy doing other things. It's a requirement that a harbor pilot who is totally familiar with the local waters be on board every ship whenever it comes into port. His (or in very rare cases, her) job is to "take the conn" and / or advise the Captain and the helmsman. These days pilots are used less and less for navigation issues and more and more just for communication. It appears there's a local shorthand in each port that these guys use among themselves and they're worth their weight just for that.

Sometime, lean over the rails to observe pilots coming or going from the ship. They arrive or depart in small gigs and scamper nimbly up or down a rope ladder or leap lithely onto the pilot boat from the ship's lowest doorway. The ladder is called a "Jacob's Ladder." Why is it called that? In the Bible, Jacob was having a hard time of it and a ladder, leading to Heaven, appeared to him. If you've ever climbed one, you'd be singing hymns, too. And what you *really* don't want to do is have that last cocktail and have to climb the ladder in a somewhat impaired fashion.

This is all very well and good, but I really don't want to get on a floating resort with neon, casinos, fancy dinners and all that jazz. What to do?

Fear not. There are other ways to go upon the sea from relatively inexpensive to totally expensive on small ships under sail or power that can take you to places the big girls can't go. This is where a good travel agent comes in. Eco / adventure cruising is a growing part of the industry.

CHAPTER TWO
FASHION POLICE

Contrary to rampant rumors, there are no Fashion Police on cruise ships. There are, however, a few rules—some promulgated by the cruise lines, others simply dictated by good taste—that thoughtful cruisers follow.

It's just common sense. You don't have to spend months assembling an entirely new wardrobe in order to cruise. Your own closet is the best place to start shopping. Your wardrobe will be new to your audience and, truthfully, nobody pays that much attention, anyway.

Ships' dress codes revolve around the dress for dinner. There are three basic flavors: **formal, informal** and **casual**. Interestingly, these terms apply to what *men* are to wear, often leaving the ladies wondering.

There are usually two **formal nights** on a seven-day cruise; usually they are the second night and the next-to-last night of the voyage. This is tuxedo (or dark suit with a subdued tie) time for the gentlemen. On longer cruises there may be a third formal night.

Tuxes are available for rent from almost every cruise line. Sometimes the men who complain about becoming penguins for an evening don't take into account just how handsome almost any guy looks in formal clothes. If there is any reasonable prediction that a fellow will wear a tux more than three times in his life, it's cost-effective to purchase one that's sure to fit rather than taking a chance on a hired livery.

One tip if you plan to rent formal clothes: purchase your own studs and cufflinks. Nothing screams "rental" louder than those nasty black plastic studs that are almost universally provided.

Informal nights are becoming less and less frequent—often only one on a seven-day cruise—but they do mean a sports coat and tie for those who hew to the line of suggested dress. If nothing else, a collared shirt with a sports coat is indicated.

The first and last nights of any cruise are almost always **casual nights** because you may not be unpacked on the front end or already packed on the back end. The later your departure from port, the more likely the evening will be designated as casual. For the guys, khaki-type pants and a collared shirt fill the bill. Socks are not required if you are wearing boat shoes. Hold the sneakers.

Let us not forget "the uniform" which may be worn merrily and stylishly by men of almost any age. The uniform is the backbone of any savvy male traveler's wardrobe and never looks out of place except on formal nights. Even then, one could get by with the uniform. What is this mystery garment? *A navy blue blazer.* Worn with a polo shirt and khakis, it's cool for casual nights. Add dress shirt, tie, and dressier pants and you're good for the informal nights. The uniform is perfectly appropriate for younger men (say six to college-age) on formal nights.

 To save the hassle of packing, my husband always wears his blue blazer on the plane. Once, when we were going to the airport from different locations, the blazer somehow stayed home alone, despite my repeated reminders to him. One would think that leaving a perfectly good Brooks Brothers blazer at home might be occasion for at least an expression of dismay. Instead, there was the spousal unit with a rather snarky smile. "I guess we'll have to go to Trimingham's when we get to Bermuda." Just as he had conveniently "forgotten" his blazer, I'd forgotten his drooling over the summer-weight blazers on previous trips to Hamilton.

Once the gents are dressed, it's ladies' choice. On **formal nights**, women can choose to go over the top with a serious ball gown or go minimalist with a simple black dress with good jewelry. Most choices are somewhere in between. As a general rule, anything you would wear to a big-deal evening wedding is in perfectly good taste.

On **informal nights**, a cocktail dress or dressy pantsuit works. For **casual nights**, nice-looking pants-and-top outfits or, in the tropics, a sundress, are just fine. And nobody will check to see if you're wearing pantyhose. If they do, call Security immediately.

What about jewelry? I have this picture in my mind of women just dripping with diamonds.

If the lady is dripping with diamonds, they are probably *faux*, with the exception of engagement rings and wedding rings. Women with the real stuff leave it at home in the safe. Cruises are a time for good costume jewelry. This is especially important if you have a pre- or post-cruise hotel stay. Nobody wants to stand in line while the concierge opens the safe so you can dig through your baubles. And you don't want prying eyes to see what the bauble count is.

Cruises are also not the time for the very expensive watches, diamond-encrusted or not. They only attract unwanted attention. It's Timex time.

No way am I going to be a "penguin." And I have no intention of even wearing a tie. This is my vacation.

That's why more and more cruise lines (almost all of them, these days) offer alternative dining venues where the formal duds on formal nights aren't required or even requested. It is, however, a courtesy to other passengers to achieve some modicum of proper dress if you will be in public areas such as lounges and show rooms later in the evening. That means no jeans, no shorts, no tank tops or t-shirts, no seventy-nine-cent flip-flops.

Many—if not most—people really enjoy the "dress up" aspect of cruising. It is rude, crude and inconsiderate to wander around looking like you're about to observe the latest stock car race somewhere in the hinterlands.

No jeans?

A neatly-pressed pair of designer denims probably wouldn't

draw stares of disdain (this assumes you have any concern or sensibility about what your fellow passengers think about your fashion statement) on casual nights or in the alternative restaurants. But no ratty 501's that were last used when you changed the oil in your car. Even if they have been washed. Also, by "designer," we don't mean those outlandish creations featuring marabou, sequins, studs, or other questionable modes of decoration. We also don't mean extreme displays of midriffs or the "plumber effect."

My husband is a military officer. May he wear his uniform on formal night?

Yes. He should, however be prepared for evil looks from the penguin brigade because *they* don't look as spiffy as he. "Dress mess" is the uniform of the day—or night. Enlisted men and women may also wear their dress uniforms. Further, if one is of Scots heritage, full kilts and sporran is perfectly appropriate. Gentlemen wearing kilts should have the answer ready for the question they are sure to be asked at least twenty-five times—"What's under them?"

Ethnic garb, if it would be formal in the homeland, is also appropriate and adds a wonderful zest to the evening's mix.

 When in Vietnam, I purchased a formal *ao dai,* the traditional costume for women. It's laden with sparkles and is past beautiful. I love wearing it on formal nights. So far, nobody has said, "Funny, you don't look Vietnamese."

We're taking our kids on the next cruise. What should they wear on formal nights?

Whatever you do, don't trick out your young sons as junior men with a rent-a-tux or even a suit. The uniform of khakis, button-down shirt, blue blazer and tie is plenty. Your daughters, depending upon age, probably have a good stock of party dresses or—for the older ones—prom-type dresses. Older girls can almost always find a same-size pal to borrow a second dress from if they need one.

How will I know what other women are going to wear? I don't want to look out of place. And I don't want to make any hideous fashion mistakes.

It's almost impossible to look out of place unless you go for the Ivana Trump look on a casual night. You can always, as one friend does, send your travel partner out on a recon mission. This assumes the partner has some fashion sense.

You're probably going to over-pack anyway, so give yourself some suitcase shopping room. Take along one outfit that could work for a laid-back formal appearance or a dressy informal evening and another one—or two—which transcend informal and casual. Keep in mind that the dress code you may receive with your travel documents is subject to change at the iron whim of the Cruise Director. Three formal nights on longer cruises could be cut back to two. A planned informal night could become a casual night.

Some people consider over-dressing to be a mistake, but that's hard to accomplish on a cruise ship. There's plenty of competition. Good taste should rule. In general, lose the gold and silver lamé, let the ship's officers wear the uniforms and avoid garments featuring anchors, life rings and jeweled sea creatures.

The worst mistake is taking something that zips or buttons tightly, earmarked for a night toward the end of the cruise. Elastic waists are more than useful and desirable. They can be salvation.

For reasons that almost defy explanation, waistlines become "wastelines" rather rapidly. After years of research and scrutiny, here's what I've come up with. The first felon is the friendly skies. Because of cabin pressurization, people—particularly women people—tend to bloat. The pants that zipped so nicely at home become a prison after a few hours in the air. Could be, too, that you don't want to wake up the people between you and the aisle if you have a window seat and just grit your (floating) teeth rather than going to the bathroom.

Once aboard ship, you don't have as much control over your diet as you might think you do. You're not in control of salting—or *not* salting—the soup; you're not on MSG patrol for excessive amounts in the carrot purée. You may decrease your intake of water in favor of adult social beverages. In any event, water retention and the associated mid-section bloating is a very real problem.

 On one early cruise, I'd planned my wardrobe so carefully around the expansion I predicted that I almost totally fritzed out when the buttoned silk skirt I'd planned for the first formal night would not button. Huh? It was only the second night of the cruise. I hadn't really even eaten anything, but there was no way those buttons were cooperating with my wishes and desires. Fortunately, I'd already dispatched my husband to the casino so he couldn't hear my highly creative cussing, couldn't see my tears, and engage in my total frustration as my plans for a fashion statement were dashed. Equally fortunately, I'd packed one extra dress . . . no waist. I ripped off the black stockings, inserted myself into plain ones, tossed on the waist-less dress, added pearls, adjusted my eye makeup (running down my cheeks) and sallied forth. Always have a waist-less, or elastic waist fall-back dress.

The funniest part? Later in the cruise as I was back on my routine of drinking lots of water and staying away from salty food, that darned skirt buttoned perfectly.

Depending upon your eating habits and choices, you may well put on a pound or two during a cruise. But it won't all land on your waistline. Be prepared.

I absolutely do not want to over-pack. Is there any way to cut down?

It can be done. First clue: *black.* I am a chronic over-packer, but I went shopping in my closet and came up with a packing list for evenings that should do for any seven-day warm-weather cruise: first, the little black dress; second, black silk pants and matching shell; third, a black silky spaghetti-strapped jumpsuit; one pair of black strappy sandals; two silk jackets in luscious prints (leave the sequined jacket at home, it takes up too much space); black organdy "tux" shirt to be worn as a jacket; dressy pullover top; Pashmina shawl in screaming fuchsia; a couple of very large scarves to be worn as shawls. For the first and last nights, I wear my "million mile" dress, a short-sleeved denim number with a high waist, that descends almost to my ankles. All of these garments have either no waist or elastic.

Half the fun of this approach? Think of how you can enjoy shopping for additional accessories or truly interesting jewelry to set off your basic blacks.

What about white—as in shoes or dinner jackets?

There is a simple seafaring rule about white dinner jackets. If the Captain and staff are wearing whites, it's appropriate. If they aren't, then it's not. But who pays attention to those old rules anyway? Captains often wear whites in the Caribbean in Winter. The white shoes rule is suspended when Winter-cruising in the tropics.

Is it OK to change into something less confining after dinner, especially on formal nights?

Most cruise lines are quite clear—the dress code for the evening is the dress code for the *whole* evening. However, with the advent of alternative, casual restaurants, nobody will ever know. Just, please, no shorts and tank tops.

What about daytime?

Good question. So much attention is paid to after-six attire that it's easy to forget that you do need to be clothed for the rest of the day, at least outside your cabin.

Continuing with the undressed theme, more and more cruise ships are featuring an increasing number of "private" balconies. They're not all that private, at least not for your next-door neighbors or, in some cases, those on decks above. Check the sight lines before letting it all hang out.

Most of us have lots of everyday and around the house clothes. In most cases, they are not all that spiffy. Our dress-up duds don't suffer from constant wear and washing. Walking-around wear is the one single area where most wardrobes need a little bit of help.

 Over the years, I have collected, whenever I can find them, matching knit over-shirts and shorts "outfit" combos. They don't wrinkle, I don't have to worry about coordinating shirts and tops, and they look a little bit dressier than whatever I would haul out of my drawers. This is a good time to take a hard look at all those catalogs that show up in the mail.

I *am* going to get dressed. What do I wear?

Daytime shipboard dining is much more relaxed, as is the dress code for activities that don't take place on the pool deck. Shorts and jeans are allowed in the Main Dining Room and other public rooms, but that means shorts or jeans purchased within recent memory and a nice shirt. It does not mean sweaty work-out shorts, cut-offs, or out-at-the knees Levi's worn with a t-shirt emblazoned with the name of your favorite biker bar.

The casual buffet restaurants usually ask only that you are not wearing a wet bathing suit, and that you are wearing a semi-modest cover-up and shoes. The dry bathing suit rules comes into play much less frequently on Alaska or Fall Foliage cruises when you're more likely to be worrying about how many layers to put on or take off.

What about dressing to go ashore?

Nice shorts (not *too* short) or pants for anyone, a sundress works for ladies, and kids just wear play clothes. Older girls and younger women with great figures should take care not to display too many feminine charms. It's one thing to offend the locals' sensibilities, quite another to excite and, possibly, incite members of the opposite sex.

Some destinations are stuffier and more tradition-bound than others. This is particularly true in ports that aren't all resort, all the time. If you plan on visiting churches or cathedrals in your ports of call, assume the proper respectful dress. And, whatever you do, do not take photographs during a religious service. Particularly in Europe, take a small scarf as a head covering. It can serve double duty as an emergency napkin.

For light packers, you can probably get by with two pairs of neutral-colored shorts and one pair of neutral pants for warm destinations. Add more pants for chillier ports. You can use the ship's laundry if "air-and-wear" doesn't work or you spill salsa on them. Just make sure to pack in a good light. The shorts that looked navy blue may turn out to be black with the upshot that all of the shirts you packed will look just awful.

We're just going to the beach. Can we wear our bathing suits?

Sure. Just put clothes over them. Toss underwear into your beach bag (in a zip-top bag) if you feel the need. You can always wriggle out of your bathing suit in a rest room and slip into the dry undies, putting the wet suit in the plastic bag.

Plan on at least two bathing suits per person. There's nothing worse than trying to struggle into a clammy suit that didn't dry overnight. For ladies planning to snorkel, make sure your suit has good strappage.

My partner and I love to get great tans. Is it OK to wear our Speedos at the pool?

Here is where a bit of discretion comes in handy. Pull a boxer-like pair of swim trunks on over the Speedo, then remove same to tan. Put the boxers back on for moving around the deck. For serious power tanners, there are "tan-through" bathing suits. Just be sure to put a high SPF on under them.

Can't I *ever* wear a t-shirt on a cruise?

You're probably going to buy plenty in port; the answer is yes. T's make fine cover-ups on the pool deck and are appropriate in the buffet restaurant for breakfast and lunch. They also provide dandy conversation starters whether you're a walking billboard for the hometown, your favorite charity, your dog breed of choice, or making a philosophical statement such as: *Give Me All Your Chocolate And No One Will Be Hurt*. You can also advertise your travels, with shirts indicating you've been all over the world. For the easily amused, include t-shirts from as far away as your destination ports as possible in your packing or put on that Panama Canal t-shirt your Aunt Ernestine gave you *before* you get to the Canal.

> **I don't think we have enough underwear to get through the cruise. I don't want to do laundry, and I hear that the ships' laundries are very expensive.**

There are two schools of thought on the underwear issue—maybe three. The third, less obvious, choice would be, "Don't wear any." Some people pack their oldest underpinnings, planning to throw them away as the cruise progresses. These efforts are sometimes thwarted by conscientious cabin stewards.

I do not favor the old underwear approach. For starters, it's less than romantic. A bra strap that torques out and breaks can make for an interesting asymmetrical look. And ancient panties whose elastic finally gives up the ghost? No, thanks. Who wants to look at a guy whose "tidy whities" are a charming shade of tattle-tale gray?

 I consider pantyhose not only anathema but disposable, as well. On one very long cruise, I was tossing them away on a nightly basis. Last night out, on our bed were all those pantyhose, washed and neatly folded.

The *Happy Sails* attitude is that a cruise is a perfect time to spiff up the contents of the underwear drawer. Even if your undies are in good shape, quantity can be a problem, especially for longer cruises. Most folks simply don't have two weeks' worth of basic underwear, new or old.

It's cost-effective to stock up on new stuff rather than pay the ship's laundry for its services on these small items. A cost benefit accrues at home, too. You don't have to run the washer and dryer as often, thereby conserving precious resources.

How many of anything you need depends upon your personal comfort level. Some women think they need to change panties three times a day. The more pragmatic use panty liners. In addition to the basics, ladies may require a special bra or a special slip for a special dress, upping the ante slightly.

If you do decide to engage in a little hand laundry, soak the dainties in the sink, then toss them in the shower for a good rinse. Wring out in a towel and let dry. There will usually be a clothesline in your bathroom. The time you lose waiting for laundry machines aboard ship (if your ship even has them) is not vacationing. Some people report that ships' laundry machines have only two temperatures: hot and really hot.

Socks, especially sports socks, are a different subject. They don't rinse out easily, they are often quite dirty, and they take forever to dry. Buy more. They can be crammed into suitcase corners (no wrinkle worries) and everyone can always use more socks.

Nightgowns and pajamas are strictly a matter of personal preference, but remember that someone must open the cabin door in the mornings to admit the relentlessly cheerful young person bringing your tea or coffee. For gentlemen, boxer shorts are perfectly modest for this activity and are also ideal for in-cabin or balcony lounging.

What about robes? Do we have to drag our own?

In the more expensive cabins, robes are almost universally supplied, *a la* luxury hotels. Usually, if robes are not supplied, just ask your cabin steward. Don't, however, decide to take the robe home as a souvenir (if you could even fit it into your luggage). Its loss will be noted and an additional charge will be made to your credit card. If you've backed up your on-board card with cash, you can bet the robe will be removed from your cabin the last night out.

All this talk about warm-weather destinations. What about places, like Alaska, which are chilly?

The Alaska cruise season runs from late May through September. Strangely, the locals call it "Summer," but tourists seem to think they are headed to Antarctica. There is no way to predict the weather anywhere, especially Alaska. If you don't take a couple of pairs of shorts along, the temperatures will be in the 70's or 80's. Trust me.

The earlier or later in the season you're cruising to Alaska, the more likely the temperatures are to be nippy. And it can get cold, darned cold, standing on a glacier.

Any skier knows that the best first layer below the waist is a pair of pantyhose. The very best are the heavy-duty support type. They provide terrific insulation. The worst thing you can wear is a pair of tight jeans, which have almost zero insulation value. On top, layer. Leave the huge parka at home. Properly layered, with a hooded nylon jacket, you're set. In case of really chilly weather, a ski-type headband takes care of your ears and the hood takes care of the rest.

While you're at the ski store, buy a pair of "Glitter Gloves." These are lightweight gloves that allow tremendous mobility of your hands and fingers. This is important for using cameras and binoculars. With Glitter Gloves worn under a pair of ordinary hardware store work gloves, your hands will never be cold and the outer gloves come off in a trice so you can zoom in on that bear or snap a photo of a breaching whale.

Is there one single thing you always pack?

Yes. I call them "wrinkle suits" as they come pre-wrinkled for your packing convenience. They are nylon, usually flannel-lined, and consist of pants and zip-up jacket. In addition to making excellent "pajamas" for long international flights, they're welcome when there's a chill in the air. They take up almost no room and can be crammed almost anywhere in your luggage. For really cold climes—think a very nasty day in Alaska—you can just zip them over your other layers. Don't leave home without one.

CHAPTER THREE
PACKRAT, THE SYMPHONY

Packing is an art and a craft. The primary goal, that your clothes don't look like they traveled in a lawn and leaf bag, is joined by a secondary goal, ease and speed of unpacking. In this chapter, we will orchestrate the process.

In an ideal world you'd have your own cruise closet and a room you could dedicate solely to the exercise of getting organized pre-pack. Not everyone has that luxury. Even those of us who do, can find ourselves out of luck when an adult child pops in for a weekend and ends up staying a month.

Desperate situations call for desperate measures. Cruise over to your local discount department store and purchase three of the over-door cantilevered hanging devices you'll find in the closet department. While you're there, pick up several of the hangers that hold a top and shorts or a skirt. The best kinds hang on each other, saving space. Don't leave yet. Score a hanging shoe bag—the kind with little shelves. And, if you don't have them in the pantry, purchase quart-, gallon- and two gallon-sized zippered plastic bags. Then hit the electrical department for a bag of cable ties. Don't ask, just buy.

Your bedroom doors become your cruise closet. Once you're done ironing, the ironing board can be pressed into service as a staging area.

Water Music

This is a two-part exercise but you can do it. Visit your local laundry and dry cleaning establishment with your cruise clothes unless they're already hanging neatly in the closet from their last visit—still in their plastic shrouds. Even if you normally do shirts and casual trousers at home, give them a treat. Ask that the shirts be *folded*, not hung. There's a reason for this.

When you pick up your clothes, ask the counter-person for twenty more plastic bags. Offer to pay for them. There's a reason for this, too. Just get them.

> ⚠ Be aware that airlines, if you are traveling by air, have become much more stringent in allowed baggage. If you take more than what is allowed, be prepared to pay—and pay dearly.

Two or three days before you are to leave, do your laundry—all of it. Having everything at hand, clean, cuts packing time dramatically. What you don't want to do is start making little stacks here and there two weeks ahead of time. You'll forget what you've stacked and mess up the stacks looking through them. Designate underwear and clothing for your pre-departure day and travel day.

Good packing is like a symphony.

Tune Up

Start the final staging process early in the morning of your pre-departure day. This gives you plenty of time to rush out for last-minute emergency purchases and permits the use of your unoccupied bed for stacking. For the average pair, this initial phase requires the equivalent of two 24" suitcases and one 26". But you may need more.

First Movement

Turn on the radio, put up the over-door hangers and start hanging. First, hang dresses for formal nights. Then, locate the associated accessories—jewelry, special lingerie, shoes and evening bag. Put them on the ironing board (shoes underneath). Do the same for each additional formal, informal and casual evening outfit. Most women require two over-door hangers for this task.

On another over-door hanger, put the tux or dark suit, sports coat or blazer with associated pants, and casual pants. Now, find the studs and cuff links, dress shoes and dress belt. Put the studs and belt on the ironing board, if there's any room left, and put the shoes underneath.

If any of these items aren't encased in a cleaners' plastic bag, use your extras. Once in the suitcases, the plastic slides nicely on itself and the small amount of air trapped inside almost totally prevents wrinkles.

Next, it's the men's shirts. Plop the folded shirts, in their bags, on the bed. Choose a tie and socks for each shirt and slip them inside the bag. Bow tie, cummerbund, suspenders and proper socks go in the bag with the dinner shirt. Stack the shirt-packs on the pillows at the head of the bed, out of the way.

Everyday clothes are next. We send my husband's shorts to the professionals so they're already on hangers and in bags, but hanging is optional. Count out men's shorts and stack neatly. Next, count out men's polo-type shirts—at least one per day—and stack next to the shorts. If he prefers short-sleeved sport shirts that you've laundered and ironed at home, they should be on hangers. Add two bathing suits, then underwear and socks according to your calculation of need. If

A sport or polo shirt worn only to dinner or around the ship in the afternoon can be recycled the next day, saving packing space.

special clothes are required for athletic endeavors, put them out now. Add a cotton sweater for chilly evenings.

While men tend to think in terms of interchangeable shirts and pants, women are more outfit-oriented—this shirt with those shorts, and so on. That's where your new hangers come in. Put your outfits together, whether folded or hung, and make sure any accessories land on the ironing board.

Second Movement

On the bed, stack your swimsuits, cover-up, bras, panties, pantyhose, slips, socks, nightgowns and in-cabin lounging apparel. I favor full-length cotton caftans—they're equally appropriate in the cabin or on deck. Don't forget a cotton sweater and a dressy sweater or shawl for evening.

Don't skimp on bathing suits. There is little worse than struggling into one that's not quite dry. If you're planning on snorkeling or diving, don't forget one with sturdy straps.

If you're t-shirt kind of people, stack 'em up now. There should be enough room left at the foot of the bed for a suitcase.

Look at your watch. If this entire enterprise took more than an hour, you probably took a coffee break.

Break out your plastic zipper bags. Shoes, particularly athletic shoes, should not be put next to your clean clothes. Bag the shoes, then bag your costume jewelry and other small accessories outfit-by-outfit. Attach the baggies to your outfits by putting the hanger hook through the bag. Your fine jewelry, if you insist on taking some, should travel with you at all times.

Third Movement

The suitcase moment has arrived. Transfer your stacks of flat-foldeds neatly into the waiting luggage—the two 24" pieces. If you're anywhere near like everyone else, one suitcase will be almost full of "his" things and the other quite full with "hers." Large flat items such as ironed shorts go best in the bottom. Add shoes and accessory bags.

This is the stunning moment when you'll know if you might need another suitcase.

If the bags are full or almost full, close them and lug them to an out-of-the-way place where they will lie quietly on their sides until you're ready to leave. They'll be available for you to squeeze in one last thing, if there's room.

Some couples advocate cross-packing with half of one person's clothing and half of the other's in each suitcase in case of lost luggage. This is not particularly effective if you are traveling solo or with someone who is not a domestic familiar.

There's no reason not to pack the hanging items next, but some people prefer to wait until the last possible moment. Start with the men's pants, on their hangers, on the bottom. The hook of the hanger rotates over, but be careful when you turn it. Sometimes the sticky substance that keeps the pants on the hanger produces nasty wrinkles that you won't see until you unpack. After that, just keep adding garments, with the blazer and suit coat or dinner jacket on top. *Voila!*

That sticky hanger goop can spell disaster for ladies' silk pants. If your silks are not just back from the cleaners and are hung with a top over them, *look!*

Sheet Music

Now, using the last bit of your clean laundry, change the bed, tidy the bathroom and set out clean towels. There's nothing nicer than coming home to something almost as delicious as your cabin afloat.

Music Stands and Other Instruments

For our non-clothing essentials, we use a 22" roll-aboard bag which I've named the **Creature Comfort Bag**. What you will put in yours—if, indeed you take one at all—depends entirely on you. For a typical cruise, ours contains:

- A portable CD player zipped in a tidy case holding about forty CDs. The CD player's speakers and power supply are tucked into a nylon **lunch bag** procured at a local drugstore. Once the CD player is hooked up, the lunch bag returns to its original purpose for off-ship picnics or snacks.
- The serious camera and associated lenses plus the digital camera reside in a **fanny-pack** case. Depending on the destination, we may include a tripod or monopod. Take plenty of film.

Make sure your flash unit and your cameras have fresh batteries. You can purchase film—usually at a reasonable price—at the photo shop aboard ship. And get your prints back in less than a day at prices comparable to those at home. Do *not* put film in your checked luggage. The new x-ray machines that are used for checked luggage are mega-powerful.

The little camera travels in the Giant Tote Bag.

- Binoculars.
- Either a small extension cord or a cube tap—one of those devices which plug into an outlet and offer three new plug-in outlets. Cruise ships are notorious for lack of sufficient electrical outlets
- International power converter
- Small flashlight with fresh batteries
- Night light for the bathroom
- Books, including guidebooks
- Small book light for late-night reading
- Self-sealing plastic bags in various sizes
- Leather fanny-pack
- Two plastic ponchos
- Two small umbrellas
- Visors
- Our own diving masks if destination-appropriate
- Cans or bags of mixed nuts and snack mix—you can't get those from room service.
- Insulated coffee mugs. They can hold either coffee or something sportier as you roam the decks.
- Photocopies of prescriptions, passports and all travel documents. This is in addition to the copies in the carry-on bag.
- Hanging Shoe Bag
- Travelers' cheques information if you carry them.

Never wear your fanny pack on your fanny. Wear it facing front or over your shoulder.

Grand Finale

The **Last Minute Bag** is another 22" roll-on. It's packed at

There are a number of packing lists floating around on the Internet. They range from the vain (do not forget your eyebrow tweezers or the right shade of pantyhose) to the somewhat strange (take your Leatherman tool kit and a roll of duct tape). Read them if you will, then use your own good judgment.

the last minute because the contents—makeup, shavers, hair tools—are used at the last minute. In addition to my husband's personal **ditty bag**, which contains both electric (with charger) and blade razors, shaving cream, toothbrush, etc., I carry four makeup bags in different sizes. Of course they match.

The smallest, the **Oh, Rats! Bag**, holds emergency supplies. Band-Aids, moleskin for the inevitable blister (put the scissors in your checked luggage), antibiotic ointment, Betadine, three or four pony-tail elastics to expand buttonholes late in the cruise, a seasick preventive, a sewing kit, ear plugs, small cable ties and photocopies of prescriptions and passport information.

The next smallest is called the **Fang and Claw bag**. Toenail and fingernail clippers (which, these days, must be in your checked luggage), emery boards, an orange stick, a bottle of the current nail polish color (in a zip-top bag), nail polish remover, high-test glue to repair a broken nail, dental floss, a topical dental anesthetic, a rubber-tipped gum stimulator and extra contact lenses.

A larger, rectangular bag, about 8"x4"x6" is the **Body Bag**. Into this go lotions, potions, styling brushes and hair sprays, body wash and puff, toothpaste and various over-the-counter products for

Prescription medicines should travel with you in the Giant Tote Bag at all times. If your life depends upon a particular medicine, double up and have your travel partner carry a second supply. Never leave the ship without at least two days' worth of your medicine in a bag or fanny pack in an original container with your pharmacist's label on it. If you go to the drugstore and ask nicely—preferably at a slow time—a good pharmacy will label these smaller containers for you. Do *not* carry your meds in one of those handy plastic boxes with each day's dose sorted out. Security people might become incredibly curious about just what those purple pills might be.

If you're the forgetful type—and we all know and love them—take your plastic box with you and dole out your supplies once on board.

anything from gastric disorders to shipboard "dry eye" and sinus infections.

The last bag to go in is my *real* **makeup bag**. When I'm not cruising, my makeup lives on several shelves in a bathroom closet. As I begin the tedious process of making myself presentable, I toss each bottle, pencil, case, tub or jar into the bag. When I use an eye shadow, I toss in any other colors I think I might need. I also take along a makeup base darker than the one in current use to account for sun tanning—even in Alaska.

If you change your lipstick shade as often as you change your clothes, put your lipsticks in the bag as you select accessories for your outfits. It's a good idea to purchase new, essential, invisible-contents items such as mascara. You don't want to run out.

These five bags, plus the **Grease Bag**—a leak-proof case with all strengths of sun lotions and blockers—fill up the roll-on once I've wedged in my international-class hair dryer (very small, and works on different currents with the flip of a switch).

The Giant Tote Bag

Airlines are becoming pickier and pickier about carry-on bags. The **Giant Tote Bag**, once just a convenience, is now a necessity if you're each taking a roll-aboard. We used to sling cameras and my pocketbook over our shoulders but now they are in the 22-incher or a fanny pack and my purse is in the Giant Tote Bag.

Giant Tote Bag contents, which don't vary much from cruise to cruise, include:

- Travel documents: airline tickets, cruise tickets, passports and insurance forms. Photocopy duplicates (two sets) are elsewhere in our luggage.
- Travelers' cheques.
- Ship's deck plan torn from brochure.
- Fine jewelry.
- Small camera, loaded, and

 I use a jewelry roll, the kind available at most good department stores. To the outside, I glued a strip of Velcro and glued the matching strip to the bottom of the tote bag. Nobody's lifting my jewelry!

a spare roll of film to capture off-the-cuff travel moments.

• Mints, travel-pack tissues and sealed hand-wipes. High-energy snack food such as dried fruits, and stomach-fillers—usually flavored rice cakes. Bottled water.

• Mini-address book or Palm Pilot with phone numbers and e-mail addresses.

• Inflatable neck cushions and sleep masks for long flights.

• All prescription medicines, in original containers. Photocopies of the prescriptions (two sets) are elsewhere in our luggage.

• Non-prescription medicine in the form of a good bottle of wine or a few airline-type liquor miniatures purchased from our local purveyor.

• A small notebook and pen.

• Books or magazines to read on the plane.

• Extra pairs of eyeglasses and sunglasses, in padded cases.

• A pair of "shortie" socks that are on my feet before the plane begins to taxi.

 For the ladies, the absolute worst thing to wear on a plane—even short hops—are knee high nylons. They are remarkably effective at cutting off circulation. Go barefoot before you wear those things. Men should lose the elastic-top stockings in favor of plain old cotton crew socks. If you have any sort of circulation problems whatsoever, pack yourself into support pantyhose before flying. This goes for the gents, too.

By this point, the Giant Tote Bag probably weighs at least ten pounds. However, it's a comfortable footrest when stowed under the seat in front of you.

The Great Bag on the Doorknob

It doesn't have to be on a doorknob and it doesn't have to be a bag . . . it's simply an early-organization repository for items that will, most likely, end up in the Giant Tote Bag, but can find transportation elsewhere. Whenever you think, "I don't want to forget. . ." or, "I *can't* forget. . ." go find it and put it in the Great Bag on the Doorknob. No "I'll do it later," allowed. The first things to go in should be your passports or other travel ID and your tickets. After you photocopy them.

Make sure you check to see if you've emptied this bag before you depart.

 You should check to make sure you have your tickets, itineraries, reservation confirmations and such just before departure. If necessary, put a sign on the front door to remind you one more time to check that you have them with you and they're not lying on a desk or table somewhere.

I ran out of room!

Note that the above packing plan requires only *three* pieces of luggage. Airlines allow four checked bags for two people. A sturdy duffel bag, preferably one with a solid bottom floor is the best catch-all-excess bags known to humankind. Flat clothing can ride on the bottom. Put shoes and other odd-shaped items on the top layers.

But what if we're going to Alaska or on a Fall Foliage outing?

Then you'll need fewer shorts, more pants; more turtlenecks, fewer t-shirts; long sleeves instead of short. Add windsuits and hooded anorak jackets, they take up about the same amount of room. If you're visiting major cities on a Fall Foliage cruise, include casual city clothes, which will also work on-board. Take along a trench coat or other citified raincoat. I don't mind looking like a tourist in Barbados, but I do in Boston.

 My husband watched once, with great interest, as I dressed for a day in Alaska. "Umm, Sweetie, you have your polo shirt on over your turtleneck." Silly man. He didn't realize that a quick trip to the ladies' room at the Red Dog Saloon would be a fine opportunity to ditch the t-neck in honor of the polo as the day grew warmer. And it's a neat look.

We're taking the kids. What about packing for them?

If they're older kids, the same packing methods apply. For smaller ones, put each outfit, including underwear and socks, in its own zip-top bag. If you run out of shirts, you can always buy t-shirts or sweatshirts in port.

We are really worried about losing our luggage.

Lost luggage is a rarity these days, primarily because of tightened security precautions and rampant computerization. In all my years—and millions of miles—of travel, I've had only one lost luggage problem, sometime during the Reagan administration. Fortunately, it was on the way home. I didn't really want to unpack, anyway, so a day's break—until the suitcases showed up—was welcome.

Be aware that the more airline connections you make on the way to your departure port, the more likely a mishandle is to take place. This is one of the reasons that seasoned cruisers often arrive at their port city a day early—allowing wayward luggage to catch up before they go aboard.

It's not nearly so efficient, but you *can* pack half-and-half in the two smaller bags. Put swimsuits and fresh shirts in the roll-aboard Creature Comfort Bag.

Other than your luggage *never* showing up—a most unlikely scenario—the worst thing that can happen is that formal night takes place before you are reunited with your belongings. The entire ship's staff will know of your travail and do everything—within reason—to accommodate you. If your sense of humor doesn't include wearing yesterday's clothes amongst everyone else's finery, they'll find you a table in an out-of-the-way corner, put you into a casual alternative dining venue or serve dinner in your cabin.

What do I do with those luggage tags that came with my ticket, er, travel documents?

This isn't as big a problem as it once was, now that passengers are required to claim their own luggage at arrival airports but, regardless what the cruise line tells you, keep those cabin claim tickets in your Giant Tote Bag and don't install them on your luggage until you have it safely in hand at your destination.

It's rare, but it's been known to happen that the baggage handlers (maulers) have put luggage on the wrong carts headed for the wrong ships. The ships are usually going in opposite directions.

I'm still worried. Is there anything I can do to make sure my luggage doesn't take an alternate route?

Get to the airport as early as possible, even though hanging around, eating overpriced hotdogs and drinking Cokes that can cost as much as cocktails may be wearing. Know the three-letter code for your destination airport and, if there is one, the connecting airport. Look at the tags put on your bags to make sure they're heading the same way you are.

Early check-ins can result, for the uninitiated, in a low-level panic attack when the carousels begin to rumble and your suitcase seems to have gone absent without leave. FILO is the rule—First In, Last Out.

I need new luggage. What's the best?

The cheaper the better, so long as it's sturdy. If you've ever followed a suitcase on its journey from airport check-in to your cabin, you know why. The airline baggage handlers and machines get the first crack, followed by their baggage handlers at the other end, the bruisers who toss the bags into the truck for the trip to the pier, the other bruisers who toss them out of the truck, then the ship's baggage boys snag them for the last leg. Soft-sided luggage has the most "give" and bags with expansion zippers plus outside pouches make more sense than unforgiving hard-sided cases. (That's where you put the smelly sports shoes!)

Our current sets came from a discount department store, on sale. There isn't a lot of room to store luggage on a cruise ship, so all the better to purchase your bags in descending sizes (26", 24", 22") so they'll nest inside each other under your bed.

When are you going to spill about those electrical cable ties?

Right now. If your luggage features adorable little padlocks with tiny little keys, you need cable ties. When your bag is inspected at the airport, the Transportation Safety Administration (TSA) has the authority to break the locks to assure themselves that you aren't packing explosives or other nasty things. They suggest you use cable ties—which I've been recommending for years. If they have to snip the ties, they will put a tamper-evident seal over the suitcase latch or around the zippers.

The last word on security procedures comes straight from the National Transportation Safety Board or the TSA. Their current information is readily available on the Internet.

Thread the cable ties through the zipper openings where the little padlock's hasp would otherwise go and ratchet them down. Clip off any excess plastic. The ties are almost invisible and will foil any but the most sophisticated attempts to break into your suitcases—unless they're the TSA. There's the added comfort factor of knowing your luggage won't unzip itself on an airport carousel, revealing to the world that you wear flannel pajamas imprinted with cartoon characters or leaping purple frogs.

If you forget to put a nail clipper or embroidery scissors in an outside pouch of checked luggage to sever the ties once in your cabin, there's probably a corkscrew next to the ice bucket. It has a small, dull knife as part of the apparatus. It works. Slowly.

Speaking of things electrical, shouldn't I take my travel iron?

No. Ships are very clear on the use of irons (except in the laundry room, if there is one), and for good reason. It's too easy to iron, using your bed as the ironing board, and forget to turn off the iron in your haste to begin the next activity. This could mean that you, just trying to look nice, set your ship on fire. Evening ruined. Cruise ruined. And some lawyers might just come looking for you.

Steamers, which use less power, are allowable but, if you use the *Happy Sails* packing method, you won't need either.

Laundry Room?

Believe it or not, some ships on some cruise lines allow you to forget that you're on vacation. You can do your own laundry! If your ship has a laundry room and you intend to use it, stash some secure plastic bags full of your favorite powdered detergent (or small jars of liquid) in your Creature Comfort Bag.

What am I forgetting?

You might want to take pictures of the kids, grandkids and assorted family pets. If you are so inclined, business cards to exchange with other people who have business cards. Perhaps you'll want to include a calculator for foreign currency exchange rates, but that's become a lot easier, especially with the introduction of the new Euro.

Will I be met when I arrive at the destination airport?

If you booked a transfer from the airport to the pier, there will probably be a smiling representative of the cruise line holding a sign that will catch your attention.

Don't play games with the airline's requested check-in time. On one flight you may be through the line in twelve minutes. On another, it may be two hours. Also, if you are traveling with a group—say Mom, Dad and a couple of kids—*count* the suitcases before you load them into your transport. Count them again as you arrange them on the sidewalk.

 I remember one woman—a travel professional, no less—who whined, screamed, worked her cell phone and, basically, made everyone miserable about a lost suitcase. Turned out that her traveling group was an extended family—Granny was along to watch the kids—and one suitcase never made it into the airport shuttle.

CHAPTER FOUR
WELCOME ABOARD

Unless you have been time-warped from the comfort of your own home to the pier and there are no lines, you are probably exhausted. The Giant Tote Bag weighs about thirteen million pounds, your partner or spouse looks like something from scary late-night TV, and all you want to do is get on with it. So close, but yet so far.

Once in the cruise line's arrival lounge, your mood should start to improve—but prepare for some sudden aggravation: just as at the airport, your luggage may be searched when you check it in.

Your cruise documents undoubtedly contained some forms to be completed before check-in. It is in good taste to do this at home so you don't hold up other passengers. Turn over your cruise tickets, your forms and your ID to the cheerful check-in person. Depending on the cruise line and itinerary, your passport may be retained until the end of the cruise.

In return for all this documentation you will receive a plastic card that looks a lot like a credit card—and that's almost exactly what it is. It's usually called a "sign and sail card" and will be used for all purchases on board as well as ID for getting on and off the ship. They don't just give those away. You will be asked for a credit card or cash against your on-board expenses.

Go ahead and smile—if you are able—at the cute young person wielding a camera at the end of the gangplank . . . even though this photo probably won't be a keeper. I've always thought it was a clever way to space out passengers as they boarded because I've never seen a boarding photo of me that wouldn't scare the horses. Photo taken, your carry-on luggage will be x-rayed and you will walk through the same sort of weapons detector that airports use.

44

If you are carrying liquor aboard in your Giant Tote Bag, prepare to have it confiscated and held until the end of your cruise. It doesn't always happen, but it may. It's better to pack it in your checked bags—although that almost insures that the TSA folks will inspect your luggage.

In addition to the photographer, you'll probably be greeted by a swirl of ship's officers and entertainers before a smiling person escorts you to your cabin. You have probably already surrendered your carry-on bags and are left only with the Giant Tote Bag. Your cruise documents settled, immediately, to the bottom of the Giant Tote Bag. What *is* your cabin number? Don't bother looking at the sign and sail card you've just been given. For security reasons, your cabin number isn't on it.

You really don't want to hold up the parade. An extra tag, tied to the Giant Tote Bag's handle, is a dandy idea. Once safely in your cabin, you can remove it. Or, you can write your cabin number on Mother Nature's Notepad, the back of your hand.

It is unlikely that your luggage beat you to the cabin. Whether you're in the smallest of inside cabins or the Owner's Suite, this is the time to pre-organize your week (or more) to come. You know what you brought with you—figure out where you're going to put it.

With the exception of the tux jacket and sport coat, everything that needs to hang is already on a hanger. Check the closets. On some ships, the supply of wooden hangers is so generous that there's no room for your own hanging clothes. Find the laundry bag (usually in the bottom of the closet), remove the wooden hangers, and put them in the laundry bag. You can give them to your steward/ess later. (Henceforth, "steward" means both men and women.)

You will notice an ice bucket somewhere in the cabin. If you are so inclined, now is the time to reach into the Giant Tote Bag for the nice Chardonnay or those little airline-type bottles you purchased at your local purveyor of spirits—if they haven't been confiscated.

If your cabin is on a Promenade Deck, immediately make sure that your windows are, indeed, one-way glass. There are two methods to accomplish this. First, and most practical, is to dispatch one person to walk around on the deck and look in. Second, but far friskier, is to stand nude in front of the window and wave at passers-by. If they wave back, or break into helpless, hysterical laughter, you've got your answer. The daytime view may be different than after dark. Check again.

Suitably relaxed, read the ship's daily newspaper outlining the sail-away events. About now, your smiling cabin steward arrives to welcome you aboard. These folks will do almost anything for you, happily and in hopes of an excellent tip. This is the time to tell the steward about any special requirements you have—more pillows, a full ice bucket all the time, an extra ashtray. Some people swear by the pre-tip method—ten or twenty dollars—the first time you see your steward. We've tried it both ways and can't see any appreciable difference in the level of service.

If your cabin has a safe—and most do, these days—now is the time to stash your good jewelry, your wallets and credit cards, your cash, passports and your cruise documents. All you need aboard ship is your sign and sail card.

For safes activated with magnetic strip cards, don't use a real credit card. Instead, use your frequent shopper card from the local supermarket chain or your library card. If it's a combination safe, use a number that's easy for you to remember and hard for someone else to figure out.

Failing a safe, or if you're traveling with a lot of money ($10,000 is the usual maximum for purposes of Customs) or some exceptionally expensive jewelry, your first stop is the Purser's office. The staff will gladly activate your sign and sail card—take the credit card you wish to use along—and provide a lock box.

Even if you don't want a lock box, the Purser's Desk is a good place to start a reconnaissance mission. If you look for a sign that says "Purser's Desk" you probably won't find one. The term that has gained favor over the past few years is "Guest Relations." This outpost is usually found in the main lobby.

Remember the deck plan in your brochure? The one you were

supposed to tear out? Did you remember to bring it along? If you didn't, ask the Purser's staff for one.

Back in the cabin, you should have noticed a little card assigning you to either Main or Late Seating for dinner as well as a table number. The Main Dining Room captains, under the control of either the maitre d' or the food and beverage manager (sometimes both) are available outside the dining room—or in another, designated, location—for changes if necessary.

You'll be finding the dining room again and again on this cruise, so make it your first stop, whether or not you have a complaint. For the truly compulsive, you can return to your cabin first and map out the best route. The Main Dining Room is usually found at the stern of the ship.

One of the vagaries in design of some ships can be a puzzlement. With the advent of two-level dining rooms it may not be possible to "get there from here." In other words, if your table assignment is on the lower level, you may have to walk the length of the ship on the upper level then walk down the aft flight of stairs.

The empty dining room means something important: food is being served somewhere else. It can likely be found at the buffet restaurant, which is usually on the pool deck. Sometimes welcome-aboard munchies are served around the pool itself. A corollary to this logic is: where there's food, there are people. Unless you're starving, now's the time to take a leisurely stroll through the public rooms. It's also the time to make note of the location of less public rooms—the rest rooms.

Nauti-Terms

There are some seafaring terms that are fun to know and fling about. A ship is always *she* and she has two ends—the pointy one and the round one. The pointy one is called the *bow* and the round one is called the *stern*. Ships also have two sides—*port* and *starboard*. If you're standing, looking toward the pointy end, port is on your left. It's easy to remember . . . port has the same number of letters as left.

It sounds silly, but in these days of mega-liners it is a fine plan to stand in the door of your cabin and repeat, making an appropriate hand signal if you want, "bow, stern" or "pointy, round."

Forward and *aft* are also useful terms. Forward is toward the front (bow) and aft is toward the back (stern).

When you're outside on a ship and can see the sky or stars, you're on a *weather deck*. If you ever feel the slightest bit seasick, a weather deck is where you want to be.

Nobody's going to *keelhaul* you (that means tying you to a line and dragging you back and forth under the ship—the *keel* being the bottom-most point of the ship) if you say front, back, right, left and ropes. And there won't be many to mind if you use the word boat instead of ship. *Boats,* however, are those large orange and white things hanging down on the sides, possibly obstructing your line of sight. Some of these will also be referred to as *tenders* if they are used to take passengers ashore. You are on a *ship*.

> On a port-intensive cruise, take a photo of the mast with flags flying at every stop. They look very cool in the photo album and may help you remember where you were.

At your first departure, your ship may be *dressed* with nautical pennants strung from bow to stern. Notice the flags she's flying. In port, she flies three—the country of registry—usually from the *fantail* (another name for the stern)—the owner's flag and the flag of the port country fly from the mast.

Those huge ropes you can see holding her steady are *lines*. In the case of lines this size, they're *hawsers*. The round things they're tied to are *bollards*. Anything that would be called a rope on land is a line at sea.

A little factoid to toss into casual cocktail conversation: the term "three sheets to the wind" has nothing to do with sails, even though sails do look more like sheets than a bunch of ropes do. *Sheets* are used to control sails; *halyards* are used to raise and lower them. Thus, three sheets to the wind—long used as an allusion for too much cocktailing—refers to three of the four lines used to control the sails on a square-rigger—are loose, the sail is flapping about and the ship is totally out of control. The usage probably originated in the British Navy as a term for either bad seamanship or just plain being drunk. Dickens used the term in *Dombey and Son*.

Many other seafaring terms: "Give the Devil his due," "The Devil to pay," "Down the hatch," and the ubiquitous "The sun is over the yardarm" have come to mean something quite different than their original uses. "Staying on an even keel," means pretty much the same as it always did, except now it refers to humans.

Getting really picky, you are either in a *cabin* or a *stateroom*, not just a room. Walls are *bulkheads*, ceilings are *overheads*, and stairs are *companionways*. For fun, check the Internet for some very complete listings of terms, but here are a few more:

Abeam: off the side of the ship.

Alongside: the ship is *alongside* when's she's at a pier.

Amidships: in the center of the ship. It's the desired cabin location for the least motion of the ocean (see *Pitch* and *Roll*, then do your geometry).

Beam: the widest part of the ship. This gives rise to the term for a lady built on a large chassis, "She's a bit broad in the beam."

Berth: where the ship is moored (anchored) or tied up (alongside at a pier).

Blast: the sound of the ship's horn.

Chart: a seagoing map.

Course: the direction in which the ship is sailing. As in, "chart a course" using the term above.

Draft: the distance between the ship's waterline and her keel. The draft of some ships will not allow them to enter harbors that are very shallow.

Knot: something often done with lines, *i.e.*, *bowline, half-hitch, monkey fist,* but mostly it's a measure of speed. A knot is a nautical mile per hour, equaling 1.15 land miles per hour. Do the math.

Leeward / Windward: Sides of a ship or an island. If the wind is blowing toward that side, it's the *windward*. If the ship or island shelters from the wind, it's the *leeward*—pronounced *LOO-ward*.

Pitch: The rise and fall of the ship, bow to stern.

Roll: The side-to side motion of the ship.

Just be careful if you see a gentleman wearing a cap that says something like *"U.S.S. Obsequious."* He will know the terms better than you. He can usually be found on the *fantail* in the stern of the ship.

Settling In

By now, your luggage should be in the vicinity of your cabin. If you were extremely nice to your cabin steward, it's inside your cabin. Otherwise, it's outside and you can haul it in yourself.

Two people should never try to unpack at the same time. If you're traveling with a domestic familiar, park him / her as far away from your base of unpacking operations as possible, but still in the vicinity. Otherwise, you will spend half the cruise answering questions like, "Where did you put my socks?" If you're traveling with a friend, decide who goes first.

Put the largest suitcase, the one with all the hanging clothes, on the foot of the bed, close to the closet. Take everything out and hang it up. Elapsed time: three minutes, tops.

It doesn't make much difference which of the two 24" bags is next up. You already know where everything's going. Put shoes, belts, evening bags and other small stuff to one side on the bed. Stash one 24" bag inside the 26" bag. Elapsed time: ten minutes if you take it slowly.

Open the Creature Comfort Bag and remove the hanging shoe bag. Hang it, and stuff the small stuff into it. Elapsed time: two minutes.

Next up, the Last Minute Bag. Truck all the tidy little cases into the bathroom (*head* in nauti-terms) and arrange them in order of importance. Put that bag inside the 26" and 24", zip it up and kick it under the bed. Kick the other 24" under there, as well. Elapsed time: five minutes, max.

Now you can take your time with the Creature Comfort Bag, figuring out what goes where and why. When you're finished with those important arrangements, put it under the bed, solo. It just became an extra drawer, a souvenir repository or a laundry basket.

At this point, you're only missing two essentials—and it's

your job to go out and find them. One is what the British call a "tooth mug"—it's a bathroom glass, more or less. You already have two—but you want one more to store your toothbrushes and toothpaste. Stewards just cannot understand the need for a third. Ask a bartender.

The other essential is "the Container." Over time, I've liberated soup bowls from dining tables and large brandy snifters from bars, but nothing works quite so well as a coin cup from the casino. The Container holds all the flotsam and jetsam which would otherwise take over your cabin . . . spare eyeglasses, casino chips, sign and sail card, bar receipts, last night's earrings—anything you want to be able to get your hands on quickly, or which would get lost or create a mess.

Safety First

Either before or after unpacking, you will be introduced to your own personal Mae West. That's a somewhat ancient term for your Personal Flotation Device (PFD) or life vest. These days, they might better be called Dolly Partons. Either way, it's all about being dramatically buxom. Each cabin is equipped with one as part of the Safety of Life at Sea (SOLAS) regulations.

The most important activity related to SOLAS regulations is the lifeboat drill. This occurs at the beginning of all cruises. Your muster station—the place residents of your cabin are to assemble in case of an emergency evacuation—is clearly posted on the back of your cabin door. Don't go there except on your inspection tour. Wait until you hear the announcement over the public address system, which will direct you to an assembly area for the required safety information speech. Pay a little more attention, please, than you did the last time you were on an airplane. The directions will be along the lines of "Muster Station A passengers, please report to the casino."

Listen to the instructions and put on your life vest *before* you leave your cabin. Take the drill seriously and remember that your muster point for the drill might not be the same in case of a real emergency. Life jackets are bulky and uncomfortable, particularly in hot weather. If you must take your jacket off, mind the straps. They're easy to trip over. Mind other people's straps, too.

I still remember the couple whose cabin was next to a muster station on the boat deck. They had an alternate idea of "mustering," to the shock and / or amusement of the life-jacketed passengers trying to pay attention to the instructions. My husband, quite the tall fellow, spied their activities first and tapped me on the shoulder. I peeked through the crowded bodies and whispered—probably a little more loudly than was necessary—"Omigawd!" Their curtains were open. The poor crewmember attempting to conduct the drill looked flustered. Why had everyone turned away from him?

Making myself as small as possible, I wove my way through a sea of orange life vests and pounded on the couple's cabin door. "Security!" I announced in my most serious voice. Undoubtedly, the couple thought they'd been busted for skipping the lifeboat drill and didn't respond. "Just close your curtains!"

According to the on-deck observers, none of whom were paying attention to the crew member at this point, the woman rolled off the bed and the man took a giant step in the direction of the window, then stopped, cold. He must have been considering the idea that he was the star of a waterborne peep show. Curtains eventually closed, the lifeboat drill returned to normal status. I whispered to a woman next to me, "I wonder if he will ever dare show up in the dining room after this?"

She grinned. "I don't think anyone was looking at his *face!*"

Once back in your cabin, give some thought to the essentials you'd take with you in case of an evacuation. Prescription drugs should be at the top of the list, followed by passports, credit cards and money. Make a plan to raid the bathroom of drugs and clear the safe of essential documents, cash and jewelry if you safely have time to do so. Otherwise, forget about it. It's not worth getting hurt—or worse—for. A fanny pack should hold it all.

Again, if any medicines are essential for maintaining your life, never be without them on your person.

 Only four passenger ships sank in the Twentieth Century—*Titanic, Andrea Doria, Prinsendam* and *Sun Vista* (*Sun Vista* and *Prinsendam* with no loss of life, thanks to SOLAS regulations), none in the Twenty-first, but others have been evacuated. Purists may argue that *Achille Lauro* should be included on the list. She burned and sank in 1994 while sailing from Genoa to the Seychelles; she was not subject to SOLAS. No lives were lost. Other purists may argue about the *Lusitania*, but it was lost in 1915, long before SOLAS, and as an act of war.

Tipping Thoughts

Any good-sized ship has a population of at least two to three thousand souls, including passengers and crew. The easiest way to sort out the hierarchy of non-officer crew is to split them into who you see and who you don't. The invisible crew are: laundry workers, maintenance people, kitchen help and mechanics.

Those you see are mostly those expecting tips. In the Main Dining Room, you'll find the maitre d', a number of captains overseeing individual sections of the dining room, and waiters and busboys (sometime called assistant waiters) who serve a small number of tables. The sommelier or wine steward will be around. No tip necessary for him or her, a percentage of the cost  If you like a particular wine well enough that you'd buy it for home, ask the sommelier to soak off the label. of the bottle is added to the check. A good sommelier—one who really knows wine and makes excellent suggestions—gets a special tip from us.

Bartenders and cocktail waitstaff are also on the auto-tip method, which may be why they're always smiling.

In the casino, it's considered to be sporting to tip the dealer or croupier after a significant win. A chip or two of the size you were playing with will do.

Do not attempt to tip the service staff with casino chips. It's a really great way for them to (a) lose their tips and (b) lose their jobs if they try to redeem them.

You'll be seeing as much of your cabin steward as you will your waiter. You can pre-tip a portion (ten dollars, perhaps?) of the amount you've set aside. This will definitely get attention if not better service. Keep a few dollar bills in the Container to tip the cheerful person who does the morning coffee service or provides other goodies from room service.

Most cruise lines provide you with a set of tipping guidelines pre-departure. It's a good idea to set your estimated tip money aside on the first day, just so you won't be caught short at trip's end. The crew who are routinely tipped make very little other money—sometimes none—and depend on tips for their income.

In general, you'll tip your waiter and cabin steward from the same *per diem* base, then half the amount of the waiter's tip to the assistant waiter. It's up to you whether to tip the room captain overseeing your section or the maitre d'. If they've performed a special service, then definitely tip them. Otherwise, it's your call.

One mainstream cruise line advertises, "Tipping not required." It's not required, but do it anyway if you find yourself on a "'dam" ship (that's what Holland America regulars call the ladies of that line because almost every ship's name ends in *dam*.). Research current tipping guidelines from cruising friends or on cruise websites. Guidelines will also appear in your cruise documents.

There are ships where tipping is not allowed—and they're serious about it. If you're fortunate enough to find yourself on one of these deluxe vessels, you'll have the dilemma of figuring out a way to say, "Thank you" without using hard currency.

On one cruise where tipping wasn't allowed, we took along a t-shirt from the Atlanta Olympics, figuring it would suit either sex. On another, where we knew all the cabin staff were young women, we took five dozen homemade brownies—my daughter's suggestion. A super-size box of Jelly Bellies was also well-received. One we've not yet tried is hitting a hip record store and asking for the hottest-selling cd.

A recent "improvement" on some cruise lines—supposedly for the convenience of passengers—is that all passengers are assessed

> ⚠️ *Never, ever,* offer to tip any uniformed officer or member of the Cruise Director's staff. If someone performs an extra-special service, sit down in your cabin and, using the ship's notepaper, write a thank you note and a note of commendation to his or her superior. You can always get more notepaper at the Purser's desk.

the recommended tipping amount that immediately goes against the sign and sail card. This approach has its up-sides and down-sides. For the most part, it ensures that staff won't get "stiffed." Staffs on some cruise lines have estimated that the stiff rate is as high as forty percent, especially on bargain cruises. The downside is the tips are all pooled and distributed by management with no accounting to staff.

You can, if you wish, go to the Purser's desk and ask that the auto-tipping be removed from your sign and sail card so that you may tip in the more personal, conventional way. There is no guarantee those tips won't go into the shared pool. There is also no guarantee slipping a little cash to a great waiter or a super steward won't go into the pool, too. Who knows what goes on behind the scenes?

One particularly savvy friend buys pre-paid phone cards and distributes them as "over and above" tips. They're the same as money, but rather difficult to pool.

What happens if I don't eat dinner in the Main Dining Room every night? Do I deduct from the waiter's tip?

No. The waiters in alternative dining rooms are compensated for not being in the Main Dining Room during that particular sailing, often on a tip-share basis with the Main Dining Room waiters.

The only excuse for not tipping the waiter? He's a lousy waiter. If that's the case, take it up with the room captain or maitre d', but don't take it out on the assistant waiter / busboy if he's done a good job.

We ate in an alternative restaurant and they asked for a service charge. What's that about?

On some cruise lines, the alternative restaurants are staffed by the same people all the time, rather than on a rotating basis, so the financial arrangements are a bit different. You still "owe" your regular waiter his tip . . . he was there, but you weren't.

We're taking our two children, ages six and eight, on a cruise. We don't have to tip the same for them as we do for us, do we?

Yes. It might even be nice to tip more. If you already have two children, you know the amount of work associated with them has nothing to do with the amount of food they eat or the amount of space they take up. The fare reduction for third and fourth people in the same cabin has no relationship to the work that's done for those third and fourth persons and certainly no relationship to the number of seats they occupy in the dining room.

We changed tables and waiters halfway through the cruise to sit with friends. How do we tip?

If it was halfway, half and half is fair.

I've been told it's tacky to ask the Captain at his Welcome Aboard cocktail party, "Who's driving the boat?" Who is?

At sea, it's probably a helmsman and a computer, working together with the watch officer close at hand. Coming into or departing from port, it's the Captain and his First Officer doing the "driving" at the pier. Approaching, it's under the direction of the Captain and First Officer with the navigational assistance of a local pilot whose job is to know *everything* about the local waters. The local pilot often issues the navigational orders and may or may not actually be "driving."

To find out just who's who on board, consult your ship's newspaper on sailing day.

Uh-oh. Our cabin has twin beds and we like to . . . well . . . you know.

If the survey done by *Cosmopolitan Magazine* a few years ago is anywhere near accurate, "well . . . you know" is an extremely popular shipboard activity. Just ask your steward to move the beds together. Thy will be done. Of course, if the beds are already together and you wish them separated, just ask.

Once the beds are shoved together, sometimes there's a difference in height. Ask your cabin steward for a foam pad to cover the canyon or the mountain range.

What if something is really wrong—like a stopped-up toilet, a broken balcony chair or a surly steward?

That's why there's a desk called Guest Relations. Keep in mind that embarkation day is a busy one, and the situation may be *triaged* with the toilet taking precedence over the chair.

What if I forget something?

You are not doomed. The ship's gift shop carries essential toiletries, over-the-counter medicines and hygiene needs. And there's always the next port. The gift shop is not open in port, so plan ahead.

 There are only two things I remember forgetting: first, a pair of silk socks for my husband—the kind worn with a tux. I realized it almost immediately and headed for the gift shop. Socks they had, but not silk and certainly not for size thirteen feet. I located the Hotel Manager, explained my plight, and he phoned an officer known for Very Large Feet.

Next, his studs. But I forgot all my jewelry, too. The stud (and jewelry) problems were solved by gift shop expenditures: two pairs of simple gold pierced earrings for the studs, a pair of clip-ons for the cufflinks.

If you use the *Happy Sails* method of packing, the chances of forgetting something are almost non-existent.

Anything else we should be doing on our first day aboard?

If you want a salon appointment for hair, nails or other beauty treatments before the Captain's gala, make it immediately upon boarding. This may be the time to make reservations for alternate restaurants. And you probably don't want to miss sail-away.

Sail-Away?

That's when your ship leaves port. Bands are probably playing, waiters are certainly offering libations, and most people prefer to be on a weather deck to take in the total sensation. As a general rule, sail-away, whether from your embarkation port or ports along the way, is in the afternoon or early evening. It's a much better time to take photos than the often horribly early hour when the ship makes port.

CHAPTER FIVE
THIS IS *NOT* NOAH'S ARK

Read the brochures, look at the TV commercials, check the ads in the travel sections of slick magazines and you may be convinced that cruise ships are entirely populated by handsome, well-heeled—both leather and wallet—couples who haven't gained a pound since the day they got married and enjoy perfect, glowing good health.

Look around you at the supermarket, the department store you favor, or at your place of worship. Are those the brochure people? No—but they are likely to be the folks you'll be cruising with.

Maybe the brochures scare people who don't fit that marketing model. They shouldn't. Just maybe there are some hide-bound people who don't want to look past the marketing model either, and won't accept people who might be a bit "different" for one reason or another.

There is no reason for anyone who wants to cruise not to do so—except for extreme circumstances. Those with challenges, however, have to work a little harder on the front end in order to ensure the best possible cruise experience.

Consider, what *are* the cruise lines selling? One word: *romance*. That doesn't have to mean steaming up the sheets or clinking champagne glasses under a full moon with nary another soul in sight. The sea itself, and being upon it, is romance. Exotic ports are romance. The fulfillment of a dream is romance. Even seeing your kids climb up a rock wall on a cruise ship, or frolicking with dolphins in port has a somewhat romantic component. That's the romance of the seas and sailing.

Regardless of what the Founding Fathers had in mind when they penned and signed those deathless words, "All men are created equal," they didn't bother to tell The Creator. The self-evident truth is there are cruisers with special needs and situational challenges. They may be blind, deaf or wheelchair-bound. They may be traveling solo or traveling with a same-gender pal or in a committed gay relationship. They may be recovering alcoholics or they may suffer from other completely invisible illnesses. They're not "brochure people."

In this chapter, we will meet some people who break the Noah's Ark and Constitutional molds. While it is nice to think—and believe—that all passengers should be treated equally, equality is not always possible on a cruise ship, primarily out of concern for safety. Physically challenged passengers should be aware that they are not always going to be afforded the same opportunities as the more able-bodied. Those who don't march in lock step with the two-by-two rule have other challenges.

Differently-abled Cruisers

The easiest group to identify, because of their associated mechanical devices, are the "wheelies"—those in wheelchairs. Some wheelies have physical motor disorders such as Parkinson's disease, Lou Gherig's disease (ALS), multiple sclerosis, or a host of other, less-well-known afflictions. Some are amputees, whether from a war injury or a nasty car accident. Others may be post-surgical, confined to a chair after a really stupid Moped accident ashore, or, simply, slower than they used to be.

Cruise lines are getting with the program and providing more and more handicapped cabins. These cabins are larger than average and are equipped with larger, specially designed bathrooms. Most handicapped cabins are situated in close proximity to an elevator bank. For the most part, all public areas of the ship are easily accessible by wheelchair people. An exception may be the show lounge. The down-side is that perfectly able cruisers, knowing the benefits of a handicapped cabin, request them. This is in extremely poor taste.

It never ceases to amaze me when people complain about wheelchair passengers cluttering up the public areas or going too slowly in the buffet line. There, but for the grace of God . . . .

It is a general requirement that a wheelchair-bound person

travel with a "pusher" companion. The single exception I recall was a young man—probably in his early thirties—who traveled solo in his motorized chair. He was "Mr. Personality" and quickly became a favorite shipmate of many people for his sunny attitude and philosophical shrugs when it turned out there was something he *couldn't* do because of his chair.

We should all remember the folks with wheels are people, too. Whatever landed them in that chair is not catching.

We're going on a cruise with my mother. She's not as fast on her feet as she used to be. Do cruise ships provide wheelchairs?

Yes, but they usually are not to be taken off the ship. Practically, a wheelchair may be far more useful in port than just tooling around the ship. Best idea? Go to your local medical supply store and rent or purchase a lightweight portable chair for Mom. In some port cities, local businesses rent wheelchairs and will deliver to the pier.

Where do you put the wheelchair? Cabins are awfully small.

Unless it's a motorized chair, it will fold. If you can't find room in the cabin or on the balcony for it, fold it and place it outside the cabin door. Some passengers have been heard to wonder aloud (read that: complain) if wheelchairs parked in corridors might present a hazard to foot-based navigation. Wheelchairs fold up to a very small footprint. Placing them outside cabin doors is within SOLAS regulations.

Part of our itinerary is a private island. The brochure says it's a tender port. What does that mean to a wheelchair passenger?

It means that folks will be transferred from ship to shore by boat, usually one of the ship's lifeboats. This can present some problems for the wheelchair gang, especially at the gangway. The wheelchair and its occupant must be transferred from one to the other. On some ships, at some ports, a stairway is involved. Short of putting the wheelie on *davits* (the rope and pulley assembly used to lower lifeboats) some creativity is involved. Usually a gang of big, strong crew members will physically lift the chair and the person and carry the entire package down the stairs.

Getting from the off-loading platform onto the tender can be dicey, even for the sober and fleet of foot. It is up to the Captain or his appointed subalterns to determine whether or not tendering is appropriate for wheelchair passengers. In general, people in wheelchairs will be loaded on to the tender last, so there's no point in trying to be first in line; you'll be placed toward the end and among the last boarded.

Private islands often offer special wheelchairs with tires that look like they've been lifted from an SUV. They move much more easily in the sand. Often, these chairs are made of plastic tubing so the wheelchair and its occupant can be rolled into the water.

What if it's a real island? Do the same rules apply?

Yes. Some ports are *always* tender ports. Grand Cayman is one because the harbor is too shallow to accommodate the draft of a modern cruise ship. The *S.S. Norway* always tenders at St. Thomas. You may end up tendering at other ports as well if the fleet in port that day exceeds the dockage available.

If we do get to port, are there any special considerations there?

Yes, more than you might think. We have become so accus-

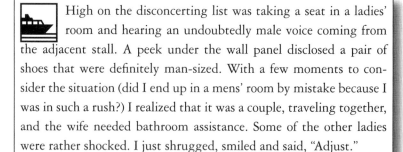

High on the disconcerting list was taking a seat in a ladies' room and hearing an undoubtedly male voice coming from the adjacent stall. A peek under the wall panel disclosed a pair of shoes that were definitely man-sized. With a few moments to consider the situation (did I end up in a mens' room by mistake because I was in such a rush?) I realized that it was a couple, traveling together, and the wife needed bathroom assistance. Some of the other ladies were rather shocked. I just shrugged, smiled and said, "Adjust."

Pam Kane

tomed to the requirements of the Americans With Disabilities Act
(ADA) that it's easy to forget that some of those sunny islands and those
ancient European capitals didn't sign on to it. You may not find sloped
curb-cuts, you may not find easy access to restaurants or restrooms. The
cobblestone streets that look so charming may play merry hell with the
pusher and his or her passenger.

**It's a scary thought, but what happens to the
wheelchair-bound if a ship has to be evacuated?**

All passengers with physical challenges are requested to sign in
at the Purser's desk upon boarding. In the case of a General Emergency,
crew members form up into pre-assigned "work parties" composed of
stretcher carriers and, depending upon the nature of the handicap, possibly a nurse. There are sufficient crew members to assist everyone re-
quiring help. Each cabin housing a handicapped person will be checked
and roving work parties move through the public area.

It's not an elegant ride. The person is strapped to a stretcher
and hustled up or down the stairs to the appropriate muster station and,
if need be, transferred to a lifeboat.

May I use the elevator for the lifeboat drill?

Yes, but it is a politeness to get yourself to your assigned location (ask the Guest Relations Desk if it's not displayed in your cabin)
well in advance of the appointed time.

> ⚠️ One thing *not* to do, for those who use both a chair and a cane,
> is to place the cane across your lap, extending out from the
> sides of the chair. It's dangerous to you and others.

Another quick-to-identify segment of the cruising population
is people with service dogs. It's hard to miss a German Shepherd, wearing a harness and walking beside a person wearing dark glasses.

There's a lot of work involved in taking a helping dog on a
cruise ship to surmount a few—sometimes many—burdensome bureaucratic difficulties. If you ask a blind person, it's worth every bit of
preparation. One of our best friends is a Seeing Eye® dog—and we are

rather fond of her human, too. It has been an honor, a pleasure and a remarkable experience to cruise with them.

Before each new cruise—after lessons learned on a less-than-satisfying, often frustrating, first cruise—the human support part of the team, usually our friend's daughter and favorite traveling companion, now checks with the cruise line to make sure that the requirements for boarding and for going ashore at every port are clear and understood. There are vet visits for tests and inoculations within a certain time period before sailing, lots of forms to be filled out and particular packing to be done.

 There are still some unenlightened nations which will not allow "foreign animals" ashore. Great Britain is one. Remember when Elizabeth Taylor kept a yacht offshore for her dogs? Until recently, Hawaii, apparently unaware of the Americans with Disabilities Act, would not allow service dogs ashore.

Our friend's daughter makes up individual binders with the required forms and veterinarian certificates for each port of call and delivers them to the Purser's desk upon boarding. The local officials collect the information before clearing the ship.

Pre-cruise, there is packing for the pup. Dog guides' diets are very carefully controlled for obvious reasons. The dog likes to have her own personal food and water bowls, her special sleeping blanket, treats, toys and—at least in the case of our Seeing Eye friend—dress up "clothes" for formal night that attach to her harness.

Never, ever offer a service dog any food without explicit permission from its owner!

Then there's the Dog Flotation Device (DFD) which must be purchased by the owner. Just as we need life jackets, so do the dogs. The dogs guide their persons to the muster station, usually with the assistance of a sighted person—either a travel companion or a crew member. But once the dog has been there, it knows where to go a second time.

Sighted people might covet their own Seeing Eye dog. It takes one trip to the cabin (escorted upon boarding) for the woofer to know exactly where the stateroom is. When her mistress gives the command, "Cabin," the dog unerringly guides her there. Anyone who has ever taken three days to get completely oriented to a ship could appreciate this service.

During meals, the dog plops down under the table and is invisible to the rest of the passengers. In public areas, when she sees "friendlies," to whom she has already been introduced, she tells her partner by industrial-grade tail wagging.

For the dog's more personal moments ("Where is the 'poop deck'?"), ships' crews are incredibly accommodating. On one cruise, crew members jumped ship to purchase flats of Bermuda grass to place on the team's balcony. Otherwise, there's a private, crew-only area for taking care of business. Exercise usually takes place in the early morning on a weather deck. Depending upon the dog and its training, it could involve four or five turns at warp speed around the jogging track or extreme tennis ball chasing.

What about shore excursions with a dog guide?

If all the forms are properly filled out and clearance is granted, the blind person and his or her dog go ashore just like everyone else. If the blind person is not traveling with a sighted companion, it's wiser for human and dog to stick with organized shore excursions.

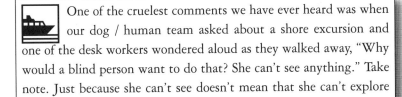 One of the cruelest comments we have ever heard was when our dog / human team asked about a shore excursion and one of the desk workers wondered aloud as they walked away, "Why would a blind person want to do that? She can't see anything." Take note. Just because she can't see doesn't mean that she can't explore and enjoy with her other senses.

Do dog guides bite to protect their humans?

Your biggest danger with a dog guide is being lashed to death with a happy tail. Don't feel shy about approaching a blind person with a dog guide. If the dog is in harness, it is available for petting after the word for "friend" is given. Out of harness, the dog's available for play.

Won't I feel funny with a blind person at my table?
Are there any special things I should do?

People conquer handicaps, lest the handicaps conquer them. A simple question, "Is there anything I can do to help?" will usually result in a, "No, but thank you." Most often, blind people travel with a sighted companion to attend to the very small details, such as arranging the plate with the meat at eleven o'clock, the vegetables at three o'clock, and the potatoes at six o'clock. No help needed with dessert.

When greeting a sightless shipmate, it's good manners to say something like, "Hi, Sally—it's Mary. We were talking on the pool deck yesterday."

I am not blind, but I am profoundly deaf. May I
bring my "ear dog" along on a cruise?

The concept of dog guides for the blind aboard cruise ships is still in its infancy and few blind people yet know that they *can* cruise with their canine companions. Hearing dogs are even less well-known. Consult your travel agent. If you are not traveling with a hearing-enabled person, make sure that the Purser's Office knows of your challenge, especially in case of emergency when you might not hear announcements or emergency signals. You will, of course, be subject to the same requirements for allowing the dog ashore in foreign ports.

Solo and Companion Cruisers

There's nothing weird about it. Sometimes people don't have a person they'd like to travel with and prefer to go solo. Sometimes married women decide to leave the spousal units behind with pizza coupons

 A pair of male friends, both devoted divers and photographers, wanted a cruise that did not appeal to their distaff sides. Their wives went off to shop themselves to death in the Caribbean; the guys went their own way and proudly announced afterward that they didn't shave for a week. Everyone was happy.

and snow shovels for a mid-Winter getaway. Other times, two men who want nothing more than a week of diving decide to cruise together. A bachelor friend often sails with a single female co-worker—everyone assumes they are married.

Often, two ladies who are divorced, widowed or just plain single decide to sail together. And there are same-gender couples in committed relationships. It's too easy to make assumptions or presumptions about these folks who are outside the Noah's Ark mold.

Those singles who don't—or choose not to have—a cruising partner just take off on their own. There's a lot to be said for the solitary splendor of having a cabin all to yourself. However, most cruise lines extract a "single supplement" of up to one hundred percent of a second fare. In other words, that sublime luxury costs double. It's a little-known or advertised fact, but often the upscale lines charge a smaller single supplement for solo cruisers than the mainstream lines. This is where a *really* good travel agent, skilled in the cruise market, comes in handy. A single traveler just might end up in the lap of luxury at about the same cost.

If you're traveling with an organized group—the local symphony, a celebrity fan club cruise or your college's alumni association are good examples— the group's travel agent may be able to hook you up with another singleton. This is cost-effective, but may be chancy, for obvious reasons.

 On a two-week Scandinavian cruise, the group's travel agent paired up two ladies who shared exactly one apparent thing in common: they were both retired school teachers. Lady number one was a tiny thing, given to lacy blouses and pink sneakers. Lady number two was built on a rather larger chassis and preferred plaid flannel shirts and hiking boots. Members of the group were sure it was a recipe for disaster. All those years of teaching must have come in handy; they did their pre-cruise negotiations over the phone, discovered a mutual fondness for Manhattans within hours of boarding the ship and comfortably went their own ways once ashore. By the end of the cruise, they were fast friends.

It's not so easy for women traveling together. Here's an example:

One dreary and chilly January night I called my friend Liz. The spousal unit was, once again, jammed up at work and the cruise was booked. Would she like to see the Panama Canal? Yes, indeed. After a total phone flurry, and a quick weekend visit to nail down all the details over brunch, we were good to go. Or maybe not.

Two women in the same cabin is quite different from cruising with a domestic familiar. In addition, it was Liz's first cruise. We did some negotiating on the plane from Miami to San José, but neither of us was quite prepared for what would happen once aboard. All of a sudden, I realized that we didn't have years and years of shared cruising experience with the resulting unspoken rules.

Unpacking in a tiny, shared space presented some serious challenges. Believing discretion is the better part of valor, I retreated to the balcony while Liz did her unpacking.

There were a number of questions we discovered; they had to be resolved. Who would have the bed closer to the bathroom? Answer: Liz, because she tends to get up in the middle of the night. Where was the nearest public bathroom, just in case one or the other was enthroned and the travel partner had a great need? Who takes longer to "get cute" for the evening?

And what about the modesty that the nuns drilled into us? For the first few nights, we carefully turned our backs to each other as we removed our fancy outfits and shoveled ourselves into our t-shirt nighties. After Liz managed to sunburn herself into lobster mode, we threw caution to the wind and revealed ourselves in ways that only our husbands and physicians had seen us in many years. Hello, aloe.

Liz loves to sing. She is a quarter-tone off. By day three, I was ready to throw myself overboard if I heard once more, "The hills are alive with the sound of music."

Delicacy and humor were required. I went to the duty-free shop, bought a Cuban cigar (Liz has asthma and our deal was that I would only smoke on the balcony) and showed her the cigar. "The next time you sing, I am going to light this thing. In the cabin."

It got better. We were on a very small, luxurious ship and there were only two other lady-pairs aboard. One pair was a sixty-ish twin set. The other pair? Two some extremely hip young PR people. Toward the end of the cruise, a gentleman who was never without his official Navy cap came lurching over to me in the lounge (he had obviously been having a high-level conversation with Captain Jack Daniels) and inquired, "You and Blondie? Are you some sort of them lee-bee-sians?"

I still wish I had answered, "No, we are gracefully aging hookers working the upscale cruise market."

More politeness and accommodation are required than anything most women have encountered since sharing a tiny room at a sorority house. On the other hand, sorority houses don't offer balconies where you can sit with your feet up, reading a good novel and slurping a cocktail. We painted each other's toenails, shared jewelry and swapped clothes.

My girlfriend and I are going to cruise together. She is a widow, and I am divorced. Will we have any problems? Will we meet any interesting men? We both love to dance and have fun in the evenings.

So far as your shipboard life is concerned, there may be some single men floating around. Whether you find them interesting or not? That's up to your good taste.

On cruises longer than seven days—and even some shorter ones—most mainstream cruise lines employ "Gentlemen Hosts" to dance with single ladies. These fellows are carefully screened for background, sociability and dancing skills. It may not be romance, but it's better than sitting around watching everyone else have fun on the dance floor.

Whatever you do, don't accept a Gentleman Host's invitation to his cabin. If you're caught, he'll be fired. Even if you get away with it, you might "catch" something unwanted.

How do we meet other singles?

On most cruises, there will be a singles' party very early on in the voyage. It may not be as rewarding, socially, as a college mixer where the ratio of men to women is usually somewhere near equal, but you will meet people who are in / on the same boat.

What kind of problems might we have sharing a cabin?

Other than what we've already talked about, the smartest thing you can do is try to figure difficult issues out on your own ahead of time and do some serious negotiating. If one of you is a night owl and the other rockets out of bed at first light, the early bird should show some consideration for the sleepyhead. And vice-versa. A late-night reader should take a tiny book light.

Think back to your dorm days. It's about the bathroom. Not just for ordinary uses, but for the sometimes-tedious process of getting organized for the evening. Who takes the first shower? The obvious answer is the one who takes the longest. There's only one desk / dressing table so you need to schedule yourselves thoughtfully. There's also the modesty issue. What's your comfort level with various stages of dress and undress?

One or the other of you may have a personal habit that drives the other absolutely nuts, like that singing thing. This will probably not be revealed until you're living together in close quarters. You will not get a star in your crown in Heaven for tolerating whatever it might be.

In any relationship, especially one in an exceptionally small space, honesty and boundary-setting is always the best policy. (This works with spouses, too.)

What if I want to go snorkeling and my friend wants to go to shopping? What should we do?

Remember, you don't have to be joined at the hip—on the ship or off. Cruising with a pal allows you to make friends separately as well as together. If you don't want to take part in every possible activity and your buddy does, just agree that you can each do your own thing.

It's quite difficult to lose your travel partner aboard ship, but it's a little different in port. One person may belong to the Dawdle School of shopping, while the other moves through shops like a tornado. Rather than the hare being annoyed by the tortoise, set a time and location to rendezvous and show off your purchases. Do this only in ports that are well well-populated with fellow tourists and travelers and only during the day.

Anything else?

Each of you should take two credit cards and "cross-card"—carrying one of your own and one of your pal's. That way, if one's purse gets stolen or a card is lost, there's a backup. Also, take along a notarized statement that your travel partner is authorized to order and approve medical care for you in case of an emergency.

Then there's the dicey issue of money. Most people have a good sense of "fair is fair." The CPA approach—counting every penny—is not the best way to go. If you and your friend enjoy wine with dinner, take turns. Same thing with lunches ashore or cocktails. Just play fair.

Also, make sure that you keep your cash separate in the safe. Using plain envelopes with your names on the outsides is a simple and cost-effective method. You do not want to have the painful experience of sitting around the coffee table on the last afternoon out with a jumble of commingled funds. "Let's see, I started out with $800, lost $60 in the casino, bought that shawl for $20, won $300 in the casino . . ." That particular exercise makes figuring tips seem like first-grade recess on a nice Spring day. One of you should take a calculator.

Same Sex Couples

A mostly invisible situation is same-gender committed couples. Comfortable with one another, they don't have the same privacy issues as "just friends" traveling together. The bigger problems—if there are any—come in the public areas of the ship or in port.

Nobody thinks much about two women traveling together (except perhaps for that fellow in the Navy hat) but two men traveling together may create an assumption in many people's minds. Though it's not as usual as "girls' week on a cruise ship," straight men do go on cruises together. Another assumption may come into play here—that they're stepping out on their wives, taking advantage of the usual high ratio of single ladies to single men. If they are, shame on them.

Will my partner and I be shunned because we're gay?

There will always be some homophobes around, just as there will always be people who are non-accepting of anyone who's "not like we are."

It's time for *them* to get over it.

What if the ship's staff treats us differently?

It sounds strange, but one of the largest problems gay couples have aboard ship is the attitude of ships' photographers. One gay couple reported that the photographer did *not* want to take a "couples" picture of them, stating that the print would be, "inside a heart." Yeah, so? Isn't that the point?

If you run across a situation like this, insist. If the photographer refuses, your next stop is the Purser's Office.

What if our dinner tablemates are obvious homophobes and *do* shun us?

It could happen and you'll know. If you've been assigned to a table with folk who are less than tolerant, ask for a table change, immediately. Some gay couples prefer a table for two, just to avoid the situation.

Is there anything we should or should not do?

Other than have a great cruise? About the only thing that might cause some negativity is going overboard in the Public Display of Affection (PDA) area. Don't put your relationship into other people's faces. What is overlooked with hetero honeymooners—even though *that* turns some people off—may not be overlooked in same-gender couples. It's best taken to the cabin, but there's nothing odious about a hand-in-hand moonlight stroll on deck or a quick kiss or hug when you reconnect after different activities.

My sister and I once took a trans-Atlantic cruise. There was a significant gay population aboard and they adopted us, much to our delight. (The husbands were at home with the kids, the snow shovels and the pizza coupons.) Among our little gang, we formed teams for the daily trivia games. And there *were* homophobes. Those folks didn't like the fact that our teams were every day's big winners and started using all the terms that enlightened people don't like or use. In retribution, we renamed our teams "Fruits Afloat" and "Queens of the Ocean." Now, that's in your face. The homophobes deserved it.

Even though it wouldn't be legally binding in our home state, can we get married on a cruise ship?

It may take some doing, but commitment ceremonies can be arranged, just as private vow renewal ceremonies are performed. There is usually a charge for the service, just as there are for traditional weddings. Charges tend to be less if it's part of a group event, more if it's private.

What if one of us gets hurt or injured? Or, God forbid, dies? Who *is* the next-of-kin?

That's a dicey subject. Take along notarized statements from each of you that the other is allowed to order or obtain medical care or oversee final arrangements. Send copies to your families ashore and give an original to the Purser's office.

Is there any way we can meet other gay couples who will be on the same cruise? Or just ask questions?

It's a big Internet out there, and there are several websites completely devoted to cruising. A couple of them have areas devoted to gay and lesbian cruising. Gay and lesbian cruisers represent a signifi-

cant—and growing year-by-year—percentage of the cruising population. There are also gay-only cruises where a ship is chartered.

In-Recovery Cruisers

Some cruisers have climbed some very tall mountains. They
may be alcoholics, over eaters, compulsive gamblers, former smokers
and others who have to fight every day to hang on to what they have
achieved through faith, hard work and belief in themselves.

For them, cruises can be occasions of sin. "Lead us not into
temptation" goes inoperative with all the seductive venues on a cruise
ship and in port. You're led at almost every corner.

There's no way to get away from the festive umbrella drinks,
the endless food, and the casinos. For those in a twelve-step program,
members of Weight Watchers, or folks just going it on their own, your
own resolve *will* be tested.

**I'm an alcoholic and have not had a drink in
six years. I'm worried about all the free-flowing
booze aboard.**

First, congratulations. You've conquered that mountain. Now
your job is to stay on top of it, one day at a time.

Two tips: Don't take your sign and sail card with you when you
leave the cabin. This only works if someone else is available to let you
back into the cabin. Ask for a glass of water in a lounge or other bar. No
charge. This is extreme.

You already know the tricks about "virgin" drinks, but be especially careful. When you order a virgin drink, if it looks anything like a
drink with alcohol in it, go to the bar and watch the bartender pour. Do
not trust a server *not* to mix up orders. Anyone who has ever taken the
first sip of a vodka on the rocks that turned out to be heavy-duty gin
knows this.

Further, there are Twelve-Step meetings almost every day on
almost every ship in the mainstream fleet. Watch for the code: "Friends
of Bill W.," with a time and meeting place in your daily ship's paper.

Friends of Bill W? I've always wondered what that was about.

Those who are Bill's friends already know. He was the founder of Alcoholics Anonymous.

When we first began cruising, I wondered who Bill W. was, why he had so many friends and why they were always on a cruise with *us*. It took a while to figure out. There are more temptations aboard a cruise ship than anywhere else, save an open bar political social where too much fried food is served and every politician is running an illegal fifty-fifty raffle. It's a credit to the cruise lines that they routinely schedule twelve-step meetings. Participants in any other support programs are also welcome.

> I once met a lady who was traveling solo; she had the same question about Bill and his friends. Since they always met at cocktail hour, she thought it might be a good time to meet some interesting people and decided to crash the party. Not wanting to be a mooch, she purchased her own cocktail from the bar and entered the room. Oops! She left a lot faster than she came in.

It does, as everyone's grandmother used to say, "take all kinds." Remember the old folk song by Shel Silverstein about the Ark? Noah couldn't wait for the unicorns, the loveliest beasts of all. Look around you on a cruise ship. There are lots of unicorns. Yes, they may be "different" by some standards, and aren't traveling in brochure fashion. That's what makes them lovely. We should all open our hearts and eyes a little further and find the unicorns among us. They may be in the most unexpected places.

CHAPTER SIX
IN THE FAMILY WAY

Multi-generational cruisers are found more and more often on the high seas. It's a good way for the family to get together and be as together as they wish. Young parents, often those with two careers, want to take Muffy and Trip along on a family vacation. That presents its own set of challenges. In this chapter, we'll try to answer all the questions that might come up.

Before you jump on that great rate—four people in a single cabin with mice or other cartoon characters possibly milling around—look at the square footage of that cabin and keep in mind that there is only *one* bathroom. The good news is that you will *never* run out of hot water on a cruise ship.

Also, be aware of the cabin's accommodations. On some ships, pulling out the sofa bed could block access to the bathroom. Most cabins are designed for the clothing and other essentials for *two* people, not

On one cruise, I made friends with a lady who looked terminally exhausted. She had lovely clothes, wonderful jewelry and a marvelously quick wit. Nevertheless, she always looked like she'd just fallen out of a clothes dryer. What was up? She and her husband were sharing a single cabin with two teen-aged daughters. The teen queens required hours to get themselves together. Even though Dad hustled through his routine as speedily as possible, the younger ladies left no time for Mom to "fluff and buff." The girls quickly hooked up with kids their age and, long after Mom and Dad had hit the sheets, rolled into the room either giggling or spitting at each other. Not much of a vacation.

On another cruise, my husband and I were relaxing on a beautiful, mostly deserted beach and were charmed by the sight of a young mom swaying in a hammock with a baby at her breast. The hunky young husband was snorkeling. How sweet, we thought. When he got out of the water and the baby was done nursing, we started chatting. The picture totally changed when a little hellion, maybe four years old, came charging up to the Mom and announced, "Grandma says she's sick again."

Turned out that Mom and Dad, quite taken by the extremely inexpensive add-on for the old girl, brought her along to serve as a babysitter. Grandma declared herself seasick before the ship ever left the pier and managed to acquire a nasty sunburn on her massive body the first day out. Young Mom ordered a double margarita, rolled her eyes at me, and said, "What was I thinking?"

four or more. "Saving" money by booking a single room could be the end of a reasonably good family relationship.

While it's just still the two of us, I'm pregnant and this is going to be our last pre-family cruise. Any hints?

Other than having fun? Check with your doctor for clearance. Usually, ladies in "delicate conditions" should have no problems in the first two trimesters. OB / GYN types will tell you *not* to sit in public hot tubs, for two reasons. First, your body core temperature will be raised, which is not good for the upcoming heir to all the family fortunes. Second, the possibility of an infection is just too great.

The stork has landed! How soon can we take our little bundle of joy on a cruise?

Some cruise lines, particularly the more upscale ones, have either rules against children or put an age limit on kids. One thing to keep in mind is the littlest ones, and even some bigger ones, can get very sick, very fast. Usually it's not much more than an ear infection, but it can scare the stuffing out of new parents. The ship's doctor is *not* a pediatrician and hospital care in some ports is rudimentary at best. To be on the safe side, ask your own pediatrician for a prescription for an antibiotic in pediatric dosage and, if you have to take the tyke to the ship's doc, be sure to advise that you have the pediatric dosage.

Will the ship have a crib? Baby food? Formula? Disposable diapers?

A crib, probably yes. As to the other items, no. If you can stand the lugging, a net-sided porta-crib is ideal for in-cabin, poolside and at the beach. Remember that baby food and formula purchased in port might be constituted differently than similar products purchased at home and could upset tender tummies. Disposable diapers are bulky and probably best secured during port calls to save a little room in the suitcases. Take plenty with you, though. You never know when you might miss a port.

Don't expect your cabin steward or waiter to heat baby food or bottles for you.

What about baby-sitting?

It's a catch-as-catch-can proposition. If there are crew members (usually young women) looking to make a few extra dollars, there's baby-sitting. On-board private sitting is not inexpensive; it can range up to ten dollars per hour. Ask at the Purser's desk as soon as you get on board.

Some cruise lines will *not* allow crew to baby-sit kids under a certain age. On holiday cruises, baby sitters are at a premium—if available at all. In other words, don't count on a sitter.

In the best of all possible worlds, you'd be able to afford a second cabin and an *au pair* to watch over the angel(s).

What kind of food is available for picky younger eaters?

All the mainstream cruise lines have kids' menus featuring such gourmet delights as burgers, chicken fingers, fish sticks and Jell-O. The older your child, the more you may be surprised how much he or she might enjoy ordering from the regular menu.

Cruise ships do have high chairs. For the smallest children, feed them in the cabin before dinner, taking along a heat-and-eat dish if it's appropriate. Cereal in small boxes, cheese, and fruit are easily available at the buffets earlier in the day so there will be plenty of finger food to take along for the tots to play with while Mom and Dad enjoy dinner.

Want to attain a high level of politeness? Suggest that your waiter spread a tablecloth under the high chair to protect the carpeting from indiscriminate food flinging. If there's a high fuss factor, take the tot back to the cabin and order room service.

How good are the programs for older children?

For the most part, excellent. The counselors are carefully chosen and constantly supervised. On some lines, the program shuts down for an hour or two at lunch and dinner times, others run straight through a late-night slumber party.

Some lines close down the children's programs in port. Others don't. If this service is important to you, know what to expect.

If your tot is still in diapers, and the program accepts children who are not potty-trained, you will probably be responsible for the changing operation. The staff will give you a pager and beep you in time of need.

As the kids get older, some lines will allow them to sign out of the program—if the parents have given permission for them to do so. This may be a questionable practice. Parents should *not* kid themselves about whether the child is ready for the responsibility.

On one cruise, a young gent just did not care for the program and signed himself out at every opportunity. He was, to put it kindly, a pain. He walked around with a deck of cards, asking people to play gin rummy with him. We never did see his parents.

What happens if there's an emergency and our children are in the kids' program?

You will be given specific instructions when you take your child to the program the first time. On one cruise line, there is a general announcement that "The Assessment Party" will meet in such and such a location. When parents hear that announcement, they know to fetch the kids. Usually, it's a very minor incident, and the stand down is issued fairly quickly. Then you return the children.

If, for some reason, you miss the code and the General Alarm sounds, one parent—if within reasonable proximity—should go to the cabin for life jackets and essentials and the other should collect the kid(s). Agree to meet at your muster station.

In the worst case, the counselors know what your assigned muster station is and will take the children there. On at least one cruise line, the kids wear little hospital-like bracelets with the location of their muster stations on them.

If you can't get back to the cabin, there are extra life jackets—one for everyone—on the boat deck.

What do you do about unruly kids?

Unruly kids probably have unruly parents. Crew members are very chary of offending the parents by telling the kids they're acting inappropriately. There's nothing wrong with stopping a youthful offender in his or her tracks and saying, sternly, that the behavior just *will not do*. This approach is usually effective.

Step Two: tell the little monster that if the act isn't cleaned up immediately, you will be having a chat with your Good Friend, the Captain. If all else fails, take it up with the parents. Look for Dad in the casino and Mom with a few Bingo cards in her hands.

The oldest kids aboard—the teen types—can be the most aggravating. They tend to travel in packs, take up residence on stairways blocking traffic and are often adept at finding someone of legal age to purchase alcohol for them. Every now and then, taking a late-night deck stroll, you might catch a whiff of something that you vaguely recognize from the far-distant past.

 Parents should make completely sure that the older teens understand that some foreign nations—including Mexico and those pretty islands in the Caribbean—are extremely strict about the "sweet leaf"—the current term for marijuana—and other substances. The authorities may toss offenders in jail and ask questions later. Some kids tend not to believe this—they've heard that marijuana is available on every street corner. Making bail for a kid or waiting around for a trial could really put a crimp in your long-awaited vacation.

What's a parent to do? It's our cruise, too!

It's everybody else's cruise, too! Be pro-active before your cruise, set limits and boundaries, including curfews. Set check-in times and places for free-range kids once you've found your way around the ship. One of the best tools going is two-way radios. They work equally well on the ship and in port.

Can four of us really fit in one cabin?

Sort of. If you have extremely young children, you don't have much choice, and they don't take up much room. With older kids, a second cabin is a sound investment. The cruise line will require that you book with one adult in each cabin. Once you're on board, they don't care.

If you stop to think about it, you probably don't all share the same bathroom at home. On vacation? And where are all those clothes going to go?

The cost-effective method is one outside cabin across from one inside cabin. If the "insiders" are typical messy teenagers or pre-teens, be prepared to give the cabin steward a *really* good tip. Also, make sure that one of the parental units has a key card to the Kid Kabin, both for security and unannounced inspections.

Now they've done it. Nana and Pops want to give themselves a Fiftieth anniversary present—a

cruise with the whole family. Yikes! How will we cope?

A useful definition of a dysfunctional family is a family with more than one member. Depending upon how your family gets along and interacts with each other, this could be a blessing or a curse.

First, designate a responsible family member (not the overbearing sister-in-law) as Cruise Director. You want that level-headed, conscientious family member who never breaks a sweat in the worst crisis and gets along with everyone. That person's first job is to find a travel agent who specializes in group cruises. With enough of you, there may even be a free berth or a free cabin.

Next, designate the brand of two-way radio that you will *all* buy. If your family is large enough, you might even get a quantity discount.

Then, let the negotiations begin. Where? When? The usual questions apply. Unless Nana and Pops want to do the choosing, which is their inalienable right if they're paying the bill.

The fairest way to do it is to choose a category of cabin that is, at least, acceptable to everyone. Those who want to move up to the Penthouse Suite can do so at their own cost—and possibly incur the wrath and jealousy of the rest of the family.

 A truly wonderful thank-you would be to pool some resources and upgrade Nana and Pops to a big suite as a surprise—unless they were already planning on it themselves.

Will you all travel as a pack, or will you have individual vacations? Will you meet for every meal? Will you go to dinner as a family or will some take early seating and others late seating? Will older grandchildren offer to take care of the littlies?

Can you agree on places to go and things to see in port? You can save a lot of money by renting a van (or vans) with or without a driver / guide. This is called economy of scale. Do pick a driver who *promises* to take more than a casual look at some maps before making port, and who isn't fazed at the prospect of taking big vehicles on little streets with crazed drivers following bizarre local traffic customs.

You will also need a Chancellor of the Exchequer if funds are to be pooled for any reason—such as van rental. Don't even think about trying to figure out individual tabs if you have lunch as a group ashore. Just pull out the pencil and divide by the number of people. But, you know your family and that might not be the fairest method. If Brenda and Eddie routinely have six margaritas at lunch and Susie and Joe don't drink, you can negotiate a factor ahead of time. Make sure everyone understands and agrees to the rules while you are still on land. Take a calculator.

There's no easy answer to this one.

Nana and Pops would probably fade away from hunger if they don't have dinner at 6:00 p.m. Bitsy and Buff want to feed their little monsters at an early hour. Some of us want to chill out and have late seating. What to do?

Do what you want. Trying to agree to a dinner hour is one step up (or down) from herding cats. Negotiate ahead of time. A nice compromise might be meeting in a lounge for a before / after dinner drink.

We're a lot more strict with our kids than some other parts of the family are. Are there going to be problems?

Someone once described a multi-generational family cruise as a never-ending Thanksgiving dinner. Think about how your family dynamics operate on holidays then expand and extrapolate. Take two aspirin. In an ideal world, all the kids would operate on the same set of rules and expectations.

What will probably happen?

"But, Mom, Aunt Jane lets Lori stay out as late as she wants and you say I have to be in by eleven."

"Sheesh, Dad, Uncle Joe gave Frankie ten bucks for the video games and you only gave me five."

"You are the *worst* parents. Kelly and Ryan are going swimming with the dolphins and you won't let *me*."

"Mom! Carrie's mother let her buy a thong bikini and you want me to wear my swim team suit?"

Take more aspirin and your sense of humor along on the cruise.

Chapter Seven
One Day at a Time

There are two basic sorts of days on a cruise—at-sea days and in-port days. At sea, the ship buzzes with activity. In most ports, things are a little slower aboard as the casino and shops must be closed and, usually, no professional entertainment is permitted. In this chapter, we'll walk through the days and dance the nights away.

Many people like to start the day with a lazy room service breakfast. Why not? You're not going anywhere, unless it's a port day. For port days, the room service person also serves as a handy alarm clock. On some ships, you receive a warning phone call. On others, it's just a knock. People with inside cabins who have no sense of day / night dawn / dusk are especially appreciative.

Traditional, get-dressed-before-you-eat, breakfasts are usually found in both the Main Dining Room and the casual restaurant area. In the Main Dining Room, there are usually two seatings on at-sea days and you will either be seated at your assigned table or in an open seating format. This is a good time to take a close look at the ship's daily newspaper, if you haven't already done so, to choose your activities for the day. You've probably already missed sunrise coffee and the brisk around-the-deck-X-times-equals-a-mile walk event. Take along a highlighter to mark up the schedule.

Even though meals are usually served buffet-style in the casual restaurant, look around for a chef doing custom omelets at breakfast and pasta dishes at lunchtime

A Day in the Life . . . At-Sea

The ship's stores are open and you'll have a chance to look at (and purchase at extreme cost) the photo taken as you boarded and all the rest of the photos that those sneaky photographers snap. If a photo is perfectly awful—and our boarding photos always are—the photo shop people provide a handy location to pitch it. You can also pitch a few coins into the slot machines—the "cha-ching" usually starts before noon with table games opening later in the day.

 If you want tresses coiffed, body massaged, or a facial before the Captain's party, make your reservation *immediately* when you board the ship

Activities range from the benign (napkin folding) to the raucous (pool games overseen by the Cruise Director's staff) and the mildly competitive (team trivia). The ship's beauty salon is operating at warp speed on the first day at sea as it usually coincides with the Captain's Welcome Aboard cocktail party.

There's no hard-and-fast list of activities that applies to every cruise ship, but you can usually expect something like this:

Daily Trivia Quiz	Fashion Show
Walk-a-Mile	Shuffleboard (really!)
Step Aerobics Class	Service club meetings
Stretch and Relax Class	Skeet shooting
Port Talk	Bingo
Library is open	Perfume seminar
Shore Excursion Talk	Wine tasting
Ping Pong Tournament	Cooking demonstration
Movies	Napkin folding
Trapshooting	Ballroom / Line dancing class
Team trivia	Casino lessons
Poolside horse racing	Bridge
Pool Olympics	Basketball

Arts & crafts	Golf putting
Tea music	Art Auction

Sports equipment available all day

And on certain ships:

Rock climbing	Putt-putt golf
Roller blading	Ice skating

Be warned, the time slots for some of these activities are scheduled tightly and everything on a cruise ship seems to start on time, if not a couple of minutes before.

Lunch follows the same seating plan in the Main Dining Room as breakfast. If you're not dressed for the dining room or hate to miss a minute of power-tanning, the casual restaurant requires shoes and a cover-up . . . the predictable burgers and dogs grill on the pool deck doesn't even ask that.

It's probably a formal night, so plan your getting-ready time carefully, especially if you wish to take advantage of the formal photos the ship's shutterbugs are more than willing to take, develop and sell. Don't feel shy about asking for a second shot if you think your eyes were closed.

For an hour or so before each dinner seating, the Captain or another officer greets his guests at the door to the main show lounge. There's usually a photographer snapping away as each passenger or couple touches greatness. A band plays easy-dancing music; cocktails are served.

 Cocktail-wise, the one the Captain offers may be the only free drink you get on your cruise. And whatever the waiter or waitress has on his or her tray is what's available at that moment. The drinks are usually weak and warm. I recommend champagne.

If the Captain seems amenable to something more than a nod and a handshake, the appropriate comment is, "A pleasure to be aboard." If it feels good, you can tack a "Sir" on the end of that.

Handshakes accomplished—if there are handshakes in these days of worry about ship-borne illnesses—the Captain takes the stage and, depending upon his facility with English, gives either a short or shorter speech of welcome. He introduces the ship's officers and senior staff and bids everyone *bon voyage*.

Then it's time for dinner. *Bon appetit.*

You can always ask for a table for two at open-seating break-fasts and lunches, but you never know whom you might meet. Or how interesting they might be.

After dinner, there are still more choices: hitting the show lounge, of course, for the evening's entertainment . . . an after-dinner drink in a quiet corner (if you can find one) . . . dancing and people-watching in other lounges . . . and late-night, the disco fires up.

A Day in the Life . . . in Port

The ship's stores are closed, the casino isn't in operation, and you have two choices: go ashore or stay on-board. If going ashore, there are two more choices: take a shore excursion offered by the ship or free-lance. Both have their charms. An official shore excursion is charged to your on-board account, the providers have been checked out and approved by the cruise line, and the ship won't leave without you if the bus happens to break down.

Experienced cruisers know that practically any excursion you can purchase on board is cheaper once you're off the ship and dealing with eager locals. However, if there's something you have your heart set on, shaving a few bucks isn't worth the disappointment if you can't manage to make pier-side arrangements.

Cruise staffers are energetic about convincing you to book shore excursions with them. Some aren't particularly subtle, hinting of dangers—including the ship leaving without you—if you choose to freelance. One way to avoid these tactics is to skip the port lecture.

In port, passengers with already-arranged ship's trips usually receive the courtesy of being first ashore. Bus passes are delivered to your cabin the night before the excursion. Listen carefully for announcements about assembly locations, when to board your bus and which deck will be used for debarking.

Some tours are so popular that one bus isn't enough. Sometimes it's first-come, first-served on the bus fleet; other times your bus pass will be coded and you find your matching bus. As a general rule in a multi-bus situation, once you're on a bus it's yours. Drivers count noses before leaving a stop and if If you're the sort of person who asks a lot of questions or doesn't want to miss anything, try to snag a seat toward the front of the bus.

one or more noses are missing, everyone waits. Usually. Don't test this rule. And don't test your co-passengers' patience by dawdling. Once aboard the bus and underway, either the driver or a guide is happy to dish local information, point out sights along the way to your destination, and answer questions.

If your excursion is, basically, a ride into town or another location, you're on your own for lunch. If it's an all-day, multi-stop trip, lunch will probably be included. Check the brochure.

There's no rule against ordering sandwiches from room service, scoring fruit and yogurt from the breakfast buffet, and putting your picnic in the Giant Tote Bag—unless there is a local rule against bringing food ashore. In some ports, that is the case. I have never seen any official types inspect tote bags—giant or otherwise—for contraband bananas.

Certain to be included in the all-day activity is a scheduled *shopportunity*. The storekeepers know they have a rather captive audience and the prices generally reflect it. Don't be annoyed if one of your tablemates freelanced and purchased the same shawl or handicraft for half the price.

Tipping either driver and / or guide is a matter of personal discretion. Some are a bit more aggressive than others. Placing gaily-wrapped coffee cans or the like with "Thank You" printed on them near the door is usually a clue as to their desires. A perfectly acceptable scale is one dollar per person for a half day, two dollars for a full day unless the driver or guide has been outstanding.

Freelancing isn't for everyone. For those who relish it, a sense of adventure, a good guidebook and local currency for public transportation are the only requirements. In many popular ports, you don't even need the guidebook and U.S. dollars are accepted for everything.

In some countries where U.S. dollars are freely accepted, crumpled, torn or otherwise mutilated U.S. dollars aren't. Mexico is notorious for this, but serious research can't turn up a reason why. When you hit your local bank for pre-cruise cash, ask for new money. Also, request about fifty dollars in one-dollar bills for tipping. One veteran cruiser recommends two-dollar bills for tipping. It's a gratuity certain to be remembered. Call your bank ahead of time to order your two-dollar bills; they usually won't have much of a stock on hand.

Probably the best resource for freelancers is the Internet. It's hard to find a vacation destination that doesn't have a tourist bureau presence on the 'Net, usually, you'll find a host of other sites by means of a simple search. Don't overlook travel areas and clubs on the various services. There, you'll find people who have, literally, "been there and done that." They're delighted to answer questions and share their experiences.

The first challenge to freelancers is transportation, whether it's renting a car or scooter, hiring a van or a taxi complete with driver, conquering a public transportation system or simply finding your way on foot. The shore excursion brochure should give you a few ideas about what you might want to do in a particular port; the ship's newspaper should offer more information.

If all you crave is a trip into town or being delivered to a beach, almost any driver will do. If you're interested in touring, it's more important to determine whether or not you have a common language with the driver. If you ask a prospective driver in the non-English-speaking part of the Caribbean, "Did you get a lot of snow last week?" and he says, "Yes! Very yes!" keep looking. If you range further afield, chances are that the cabbies who ply the ports will have English. After all, they're looking for a good tip.

Arranging to share a van or a cab with others is cost-effective—half the price or less—and double or more the fun. Just make sure you've negotiated the price ahead of time and that the driver understands he or she will be paid once you're safely back at the pier.

Don't let your driver tell you that you must do one thing or another. If you don't want to visit the rope factory or the alligator hatchery—even if they are the pride of the island—just say so. Your shipmates on the planned excursions have to suffer through them—you don't. A good general plan is to ask the driver for an orientation tour first. Then you can decide what to do next—go back to the falls, hit the third beach along the way, or visit that little craft market next door to the church you also want to look at.

When you scatter—shopping, for example—make sure everyone has a watch and knows the rendezvous place and time. The very best drivers find a place to sit nearby the meeting spot and are available to you for serious shopping negotiations if there's a language barrier with a vendor.

> ⚠️ One important thing to remember is that the local time in port may not be the same time that's on the ship's clock. This can happen when your ship changes time zones for only one day. Look at the phone in your room. Does it display the time? That's the time the ship thinks it is, regardless of what the clocks ashore may say. There are also clocks all over the ship.

If you've hired your driver for the day, you will probably stop for lunch. It's a courtesy to invite your driver to join you and pick up his tab. It's highly unlikely that your offer will be accepted but, if you've all been getting along famously, you may insist and your driver might happily agree. Don't be quite so generous with your invitation if you're stopping for a serious margarita fix. Most drivers choose to hang with their friends while you're enjoying your meal or drinks.

Back at the ship, it's time to shower off the sand and shopping dust before dinner—generally a casual night if the port stop was long, possibly informal if sail-away is an early one.

Maybe you've been to a port twenty times before. Maybe the port doesn't interest you. Maybe you have a cold or an attitude and just plain want to stay in one place. The pace of activities aboard slows to a crawl once almost everyone else has gone ashore. It's not impossible that the Main Dining Room will be closed and the only lunch available will be in the casual restaurant or on the pool deck. You are not required to get off the ship. More importantly, especially if traveling with a domestic partner, is that you don't have to be joined at the hip. You aren't linked together at home, why on a cruise? If one person really wants to laze around and the other is hot for hiking to the top of the local volcano, laze on and hike on. It will give you fodder for dinner conversation.

Are the ship's shore excursions really a rip-off?

Most emphatically, *no*. They are generally more expensive than an almost identical tour you can pick up on the pier, but have several advantages. You are with a ship-sponsored group at all times, the service is door-to-door, everything is done for you, all you have to do is get on and off the bus. The comfort and security level is high; that's important to a lot of people. And the ship really won't leave without you.

What if the ship does leave without us? We want to freelance.

The smartest thing to do is make sure your plans include the worst possible thing that could happen as far as possible from the ship . . . then build that time into your return schedule. Drivers are particularly sensitive to time constraints. And remember that the ship's clock *is* the ship's clock.

Other than parting with a lot of cash, rejoining the ship from a small boat alongside is not for the faint of heart. If you've ever watched the harbor pilots shinny up that rope ladder, that's how you have to board. No gangplanks at sea.

Alternate Plan B is to stay overnight and charter an airplane or catch a commercial flight to meet your ship at the next port. It's a good idea to have a clue as to the next port.

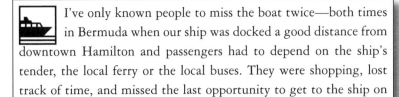 I've only known people to miss the boat twice—both times in Bermuda when our ship was docked a good distance from downtown Hamilton and passengers had to depend on the ship's tender, the local ferry or the local buses. They were shopping, lost track of time, and missed the last opportunity to get to the ship on time.

Not surprisingly, in each instance there was a gentleman with a fast boat who offered—for a significant sum of money—to catch the ship. We always wondered whether or not he took credit cards.

Another time, friends relied on local clocks and were dashing up the gangway with milliseconds to spare.

What if we want to tour around, then go to a beach, then go shopping all in the same day?

Get an early start. Women can wear a sundress or other accommodating outfit over bathing suits, underwear (in a zip-top bag) goes into the Giant Tote Bag. Men can wear a shirt and a bathing suit —so long as it's not a Speedo type—with shorts and underwear also in the Giant Tote Bag. Wet bathing suits go into the zip-top bags that held the dry clothes. Don't forget the suntan lotion, either the entire Grease Bag or the SPF *du jour*.

How do we get beach towels?

The ship provides them, signed out to your cabin account. Either you order them from your cabin steward, they show up in your stateroom or you collect them as you debark. If you lose one, you'll find out just how expensive plain, large towels can be. Don't be shy about asking for more than one.

Anything else?

Sunglasses, visor, a hairbrush to share, wet-wipes for hands, small pack of tissues in case of ill-equipped restrooms, bottled water and your official ship's ID card.

Is there any way of telling which portside driver is the best?

They all are—just ask them. In some ports, there are drivers with a local official designation, which usually indicates their vehicle is safe and they have either attended or passed a course on guiding. Look for a sticker in the window or on the license plate. Even better, ask your Cruise Director what to look for before you get off the ship.

Why should we pay a driver to hang around all day if all we're going to do is go to the beach?

Don't. Just make sure you set a time for him to pick you up for the return journey if you're worried that another cab might not come along. He'll probably insist on payment when he drops you off; that's only fair. Sometimes people change their minds and find other transportation back to the ship.

What should we do with our ship's cards and money if we want to swim or snorkel?

"Water wallets" are available from luggage stores and, usually, in the ship's gift shop. They hang around your neck.

But what about my camera?

Look around you. There will undoubtedly be some respectable-looking people sharing sand with you. Ask nicely if they would mind keeping an eye on it. This does require a certain amount of trust.

What about tips for private drivers?

Nice, but not necessary if they own their own vehicles and are self-employed.

What happens if I forget my ship's ID card?

Most cruise lines check for them as you debark, which lessens the chances of forgetting. But if you do forget—or it's lost or stolen—you will not be denied boarding. Instead, you will become one of the security staff's new best friends while they check your *bona fides*.

> But I am *extremely* forgetful and disorganized. My spouse and children are worse. I don't want to spend the whole cruise getting cards replaced.

This is so simple it's almost stupid, but I have been known to do it. Take along *extremely* long shoelaces and a standard hole-punching device. (Pack it in your checked luggage—it could freak out a security person.) Punch a hole in each card (avoid the magnetic strip, please), and wear your card around your neck.

CHAPTER EIGHT
EAT, DRINK AND BE MERRY

If there's a single concept synonymous with the word *cruise*, it's probably more likely to be *food* than *water*. The first question civilians and experienced cruisers ask when you return home is, "How was the food?" Years of reading cruise reviews on the Internet bear this out—more space is given to describing and critiquing meals than any other part of the cruise experience.

Most women who cruise haven't looked like the skinny chicks in the bikinis or high-cut bathing suits who appear in cruise line commercials since the days of prom dresses. Their escorts? They are certainly not the buff guys we ladies see on TV since the husband discovered beer, popcorn (with butter) and Sunday afternoon football.

The Cruise Diet

You heard it here first. A cruise is a great opportunity to knock off a bit of that excess poundage. Don't panic. You're not about to hear any suggestions that you spend two or three hours a day in the Purgatory known as the spa, which is little more than an assembly of high-tech instruments of physical torture.

Before we get into how to lose weight, let's think about going the other way: gorging. There's the Sir Edmund Hilary approach. "It is there, I must eat it." There is a corollary, "I paid for it, I must eat it." The truth is, most of us are not accustomed to food being available twenty-four / seven and are afforded few opportunities to participate in the sin of gluttony.

If you routinely nosh a bagel and slurp down a cup of coffee for breakfast, leave the Eggs Benedict alone. Well, except for maybe once.

If lunch is usually soup and salad, you really don't want those elaborate casseroles, the thick slices of roast beef and ham, plus those utterly tempting desserts. For most of us, the word *tea* means a little white bag that you toss in a cup with boiling water, not cunning little sandwiches and seductive desserts. How many of us have five-course dinners at home every night? If you're not married to a professional dessert chef, a midnight buffet of sixty-two kinds of chocolate creations is an unlikely part of life. And most of us don't have a self-serve soft ice cream or frozen yogurt machine in the kitchen.

Then there's the cocktailing. Liquor has calories—lots of them. Those sailing in Summer or to warmer climes in the Winter who would never consider drinking anything but diet cola with their rum, latch on to the refreshing tonic (quinine water) drinks. Tonic has more calories than regular cola. The "foo-foo" drinks, always adorned with umbrellas, look pretty, taste great, and pack a serious calorie punch—whether they have liquor in them or not—belied by their benign appearance.

Now that we know the diet danger zones (i.e., almost everywhere), here's the combat plan:

🐬 Drink plenty of water. Long air flights, diet and lifestyle changes contribute severely to dehydration, which results in water retention and bloating, which makes you feel as though you have gained weight. The water on cruise ships is completely potable and probably safer than the water that comes out of your spout at home.

 Even though nobody fancies spending half the cruise in a rest room, becoming dehydrated is a serious issue. Doctors will tell you to parse the potty—check the color of your urine. A dark color other than first thing in the morning signals dehydration.

🐬 Order a double carafe of coffee from room service first morning out and hide the carafe. Use it to keep cold water available at all times.

🍴 If you don't take an over-the-counter or prescription diuretic, cucumbers and melons are excellent for releasing excess fluids should you "puff up."

🍴 Walk, don't run. On most cruises you will have the opportunity to walk a mile or so with an extremely perky young person around breakfast time each day. Regular participation will usually result in a natty t-shirt certifying that you're some sort of health nut.

🍴 Avoid salty foods (bar snacks) at all costs.

🍴 Whenever possible, take the stairs rather than the elevators. Walking up is better for you than walking down.

🍴 Plan your meals, especially dinner, carefully. Don't order anything that you could enjoy at a shoreside restaurant in a better presentation than on-board. Most ships post the evening's menu somewhere around lunchtime. Read the dinner menu before deciding on lunch. Take a close took at the "Light and Healthy" or "Lean and Mean" choices.

🍴 Walk the line. Before loading up your plate at any buffet, walk behind the plate-loading patrons—peek politely over their shoulders or between them and decide on your meal. Don't start loading your plate and keep on loading. Look it all over and make a careful decision.

🍴 Pool deck lunches are death to even the most carefully planned diets. Ah, the smell of those burgers. And you *do* want fries with that? Those burgers, though, usually smell better than they taste. Regulations require that they're cooked almost to death and usually end up tasting like sawdust with ketchup and pickles.

🍴 Some of the best food offerings at sea are the appetizers. They're usually the first thing made in the morning when the chef's staff can devote more time to them. The servings are usually small and, often, quite delicious—food you're not likely to have at home. Cruises are a time to be adventurous.

🍴 Take more time talking to your tablemates than stuffing your face. Consider the breadbasket to be a décor item. Eat slowly.

🍴 Only eat half of the entrée if, indeed, you do choose an en-trée. (I usually have two appetizers, light soup, a salad and dessert.) Practice in the bathroom mirror at home how to respond to the waiter who says, "But you deed not like eet?" "I'm just saving room for dessert," is an excellent answer. Explaining to your waiter early on that you *just don't eat everything* should keep him out of your face.

🍴 Do not even *think* about having a second entrée, even though they are readily available. However, *tasting* three different desserts is not a sin.

🍴 Remember that you may be more active on a cruise than you are at home, especially if you are desk-bound. In European or other exotic ports you may not even realize how much you're walking; in warm-water destinations, change that to swim and float.

🍴 If you're a second-seating type, order some fruit and cheese from room service to take the edge off, so you're not starving when you make it to table.

🍴 Nibble. A little bit here, a little bit there will keep the stomach happy. Just choose your nibbles carefully.

🍴 Carry zip-top bags with you. When you see a display of healthy food such as fruit or vegetables, snag some to take back to your cabin. It is considered to be un-cool to load the bags at the buffet. Put the produce on your plate and fill the plastic discreetly at your table.

🍴 If you're spending the day ashore, gather healthy foods such as fruits, vegetables, and yogurt from breakfast and pack them into the little insulated lunch pack you take with you. Far better than two bags of chips. And remember, you are *not* stealing.

🍴 "Fried" is a four-letter word.

🍴 A cruise is one of the few times in life when you really *have* a choice. Keep it in mind.

🍴 If all else fails, carry along a few pony-tail holders. They are great waistline expansion devices.

Bon Appetit! Just not too much of it.

The Main Dining Room

Traditionally the centerpiece of shipboard cuisine, the Main Dining Room, defines the overall quality of the dining experience. When a cruiser says, "Dinners were fine, but breakfast and lunch didn't do much for me," it's a good bet that cruiser didn't take those meals in the Main Dining Room.

There's nothing to stop you from taking a stroll through the dining room while it's empty to check out the location of your assigned table.

The Main Dining Room is a quiet land of floral arrangements, soft music, glittering crystal, tasteful china, shining silver and enough linen to cover your average football field. It's also the place where more staff competes for your tip dollar than anywhere else on the ship—your room steward comes in a distant second.

There's a strict staff / crew hierarchy that varies slightly from cruise line to cruise line. As an example, the staff captain reports to the captain. the hotel manager reports to the staff captain. The maitre d' reports to the hotel and restaurant manager. Room captains report to the maitre d', waiters serve under the watchful eye of room captains, and busboys—or assistant waiters—serve, in turn, the waiters.

Your first visit to the Main Dining Room will, predictably, be a bit chaotic as everyone finds the proper table for the first time. Don't forget your table assignment card. And, if you wish to look every bit the world cruiser, wait about ten minutes from the time the meal is called to enter the dining room. The staff will be grateful that you're not part of the initial flesh press and you'll have a moment to make a good first impression, which will serve you well as the cruise goes on.

Now for the fun part. If you're seated at anything but a table for two—a four, a six, an eight, a ten—will your tablemates be friends or enemies? Most cruisers enjoy meeting new people—breaking bread together is one of the best ways to get to know others. Breaking the rules of good manners isn't.

There's no delicate way to say it. Sometimes you'll be saddled

We were once seated at a table for four with a couple from Paris. They had very little English, my husband's high school French was just that, and I was in another country entirely. The first night's dinner was extremely awkward and, we found out later, both couples considered asking for a change of table. As it turned out, the four of us dined with the Captain the next night—putting off the decision—and, after enough wine, their English and my husband's French improved dramatically. We swapped addresses at the end of the cruise.

with tablemates who offend your sensibilities for one reason or another. Maybe it's wardrobe, maybe it's hygiene or maybe it's boorish behavior. Perhaps you simply have nothing in common. If they're drinking beer and talking about motorcycles and you're drinking wine and discussing Restoration novels, there may be a bit of tension around the groaning board. The cure is a visit to the maitre d', preferably with a neatly folded bill (a ten- or twenty-dollar bill) in your pocket to pass—with extreme discretion—into his waiting hand. But there are other sorts of mis-fits.

 On one cruise, sail-away was very late, so the first night's dinner was open seating. We ended up at a table for eight. Two of the couples were wide-eyed first-time cruisers. My husband and I were exhausted after a long flight and several hours spent inspecting two new ships that were in harbor that day. One fellow immediately took charge of the table conversation, announcing his and "the wife's" names, how many cruises they'd been on, and so on. Then he asked the rest of the table to respond. Feeling rather like I'd returned to elementary school, I mumbled "Housewife, not very many" and my husband offered up, "Semi-retired, a couple less than my wife has been on."

Mr. Brasso saw his opportunity to be a star and impress the heck out of the rest of us with a lengthy monologue about his cruising experiences, the foreign countries where he'd lived, and any other odd pieces of information he could dish up. The first-time cruisers just stared.

My patience, when I'm tired, is limited. My husband gave

me the well-known "Down, Girl!" look, but it was too late. With a sweet smile I asked, "And were you an *officer* in the military?"

My husband, attempting to derail a confrontation that was sure to escalate, spilled the beans about my career as a travel writer, the number of countries we'd visited, and how many cruises we'd taken.

This was an error of judgment. Brasso and "the wife" decided they had hit the jackpot and had to be our new best friends. We spent a good part of the cruise saying, "No, thank you," to offers of drinks, spending time on deck ("We'll save lounge chairs for you,") and going on shore excursions together. Brasso went so far as to ask if I could arrange for him and "the wife" to be invited to the Captain's table and have tours of the bridge and the engine room.

It's also possible that you'll be the victim of the Waiter From Hell. There's at least one in every dining room and the maitre d's staff knows which ones. They tend to serve tables closer to the center—thus, under watchful eyes at all times—and serve less tables. This dining room Lucifer may be brand-new and unsure of what he's doing. He may be on his last or next-to-last cruise under his current contract and can't wait to get home. He may have broken up with his shipboard lover or received a letter from home that made him unhappy. Who knows?

You do not have to tolerate the Waiter From Hell.

This request for a change does not require taking a financial offering to the maitre d'. He should give you money for pointing out problems in his dining room. Don't pull any punches. Explain what the waiter did or didn't do that drove you to such extreme measures. Not only will the waiter be reprimanded, he'll lose your tip money, which probably hurts even worse.

Personally, I tend to cut new waiters a bit of a break, but won't tolerate the surly or those with other attitude problems. I'm also sympathetic to the busboys who, because of their waiter "boss," miss out on tippage. On a jam-packed cruise where a waiter station move wasn't possible, the Room Captain served our table and the busboy received both the waiter's tip and his own. Remember the busboy—he doesn't deserve punishment, even if the waiter does.

Let's assume that you find your tablemates convivial and your waitstaff ready, willing and able to make your dining experience the best ever. There are still a couple of wrinkles that may need ironing. If half the table starts standing in line ten minutes before the doors open and the other half lingers over pre-dinner cocktails and shows up ten minutes after, there could be a problem.

Being first in the Main Dining Room gains you relatively little—the kitchen works on its own schedule. As a general rule, waiters are *not* going to start serving part of the table, particularly if it's a larger one, until all souls are present and accounted for. Nor will they begin until the appointed door-closing moment—usually fifteen minutes after the scheduled seating. They'll take orders, but they won't turn them in to the kitchen or serve. Do the experienced cruiser thing with your tablemates and suggest that everyone agree to come to table five minutes late, maybe getting together for cocktails first.

People tend to come to the dining room for the first dinner *a la* Noah's Ark—two by two. Then they sit down two by two, partner with partner—and do the same thing the whole cruise, including the same chairs. *Boring.* Take the lead on the first night and suggest changing seating arrangements with the dessert course. Experienced cruisers will often split up when they come to table, paving the way for others to do the same.

Another dicey area is the subject of wine at the table. It seems rude to order a bottle of wine for just the two (or one, if you are a solo cruiser) of you, and not share with the others, doesn't it? Stop! Would you offer the others a sip of your cocktail? Probably not. Keep that in mind. To make your position perfectly clear, you might ask, "Is anyone else ordering wine?" Or, "We're ordering the Cakebread Cellars Chardonnay. What are you having?"

 Once upon a cruise we shared an extremely convivial table and discovered a very reasonably-priced Chardonnay that everyone liked. The sommelier was instructed to keep the wine flowing and to rotate charging the cabins. This is unusual.

The silver on the table isn't yours to keep, but it may be an array such as you've never seen before. Even if you have seen silver in profusion on other occasions, you may be baffled as to the arrangement before you.

The big plate in the center is called a *place plate* or *charger*. It's larger than a dinner plate and is the landing space for your appetizer, soup and salad. It's removed before your entrée arrives. The plate to the upper left of that is your bread and butter plate. The butter knife is usually on the bread and butter plate but may be to the right of the place plate. To the upper right are glasses for water, red wine and white wine. Depending on your order, one or both wine glasses will be removed.

Someone will probably appropriate the wrong bread and butter plate. This is a moment of embarrassment for the person who used the wrong plate and a moment of breadlessness for the person who comes up short. Rather than announcing, loudly, your lack of a plate, *quietly* ask the waiter for another.

To the left are two—maybe three—forks: a salad fork outside and a dinner fork inside. To the right are at least a soupspoon, a place spoon, and a dinner knife. Often, a dessert spoon and fork are placed above the place plate.

The universal signal that you've finished a course is to place your silverware (tines or bowl down for forks and spoons) in a position with the "tops" of silverware pointing toward "eleven" and the handles pointing toward "five," as if your plate were a clock face.

If your appetizer (first course) requires a special fork or other instrument—such as a cocktail fork for shrimp or other seafood—it will be presented with your food. If the appetizer can be attacked with a normal salad-type fork, use the one on the table, placing it on the serving plate when you're done. Only a sloppy waiter will put the fork back on the table; it should be replaced before the salad course.

The soupspoon isn't hard to figure out; neither is the salad fork. Some appetizer courses and some salads require the use of your dinner knife. Again, put them on the serving plate and expect them to be carried away, then replaced.

If you order fish for dinner, you may well be presented with a special knife and fork called a fish service. Roasts or steaks bring along a sharper-edged knife.

The easy way to tame your silverware is to remember that you always work from the outside, in. If you goof, a good waiter will notice and, unobtrusively, replace the piece.

Unless you're a serious foodie—and, maybe, even if you are—there are menu items which seem designed to confuse and are almost impossible to decode without a copy of *Larousse* at your side. Fortunately, most cruise lines offer a translation or the waiter can tell you that the *entrêcote de boeuf aux champignons* is steak with mushrooms. You always order from the menu in the Main Dining Room.

Most cruise lines also offer non-menu items—a grilled steak, a baked chicken breast—if you just can't abide any of the evening's offerings. A cruising friend has an obsession with mashed potatoes. The first night of each cruise, he tells the waiter he wants mashed potatoes *every* night. He gets them.

> On some cruise lines, you need to order tomorrow's Eggs Benedict today. Check to make sure.

Breakfast is fairly straightforward. Juice and coffee appear immediately. You have the opportunity for more fruit (are Kadota figs served anywhere except on cruise ships?), eggs a number of ways, pancakes or waffles, potatoes, specialty dishes such as Eggs Benedict and a variety of breakfast meats.

Lunch can easily stretch to four courses with an appetizer, soup or salad, entrée, and dessert. There's no requirement to choose something from each stanza of the menu at lunch, or for that matter, ever.

At dinner time, course work is the rule. First, there's an appetizer. Then soup appears. Followed closely by the salad. Then comes your entrée. Then, that too-tempting dessert arrives. That makes five courses—at least. On formal nights, there may also be a sorbet course. Celebrity, generally considered tops for food among the mainstream cruise lines, offers five or six appetizers, three soups, two or more salads, and seven entrees each night at dinner. You won't find quite as many offerings on other cruise lines, but you can count on a fish, a poultry, a beef, either pork or veal, and pasta, whether as an appetizer or a main course. You can also count on lighter choices. The menu contains the chef's suggestions for the entire meal as well as the recommended low-cal, low-fat choices.

You heard it here first. A cruise is the time to eat adventurously. If you don't like it, send it back and order something else. If you do like it, you've just expanded your gustatory horizons.

To the consternation of the international food specialists who design shipboard cuisine, Americans' tastes aboard ship are not particularly adventurous. In the course of one interview, an executive chef vented. "*Lo-abster* and steak. Steak and *lo-abster*. And those % ^ @ # shreemp coaktails."

In another interview, I took a highly-placed Celebrity official to task for removing my absolutely favorite appetizer, quail paté, from the menu. "But I loved it. I always had two servings."

"You and three other passengers, Madame." He went on, very smoothly, to assure me that I would adore the replacement, *mousseline* of *phay-zant*. Phay-zant? Oh, pheasant. It was OK. Pleasant pheasant.

You need not be a slave to the menu. If you prefer a plain plate of boring iceberg lettuce rather than crunched-up romaine or hip, sexy meszclune, tell your waiter. You'll have it.

But be careful what you ask for, you'll keep getting it—and getting it—and getting it. Waiters take great pride in their memories for special requests. If you order iced tea or milk with dinner the first night out, it will appear—as reliably as sunset—at your place for the rest of the cruise unless you make it clear it was a one-time-only request. One request that never seems to sink in is milk, rather than cream, for coffee.

The more dedicated a cruise line is to family-oriented travel, the greater the variety of items on special children's menus. Think chicken fingers, pizza, spaghetti, burgers and dogs. But the kids may surprise you by ordering from the regular menu and enjoying their choices.

Cruises are ideal venues for vegetarians. They'll find a far greater selection of meat-free meals than most "regular" restaurants offer. Folks who eschew (and don't chew) red meat will be in white-meat heaven. Hard-line vegans probably should forego a diet of cruise food.

If you are on a special diet for a health condition—diabetes is the most common dietary concern—make your needs known to your travel agent when you book your cruise. And make sure the travel agent gets a response from the cruise line as to exactly how accommodating they are. You may need to carry some of your own food items, such as salad dressings, jams and syrups, if they are important to you.

It is possible to keep kosher on a cruise ship. It may not be too interesting—but possible, it is. Kosher foods are boarded frozen and thawed out as the cruise progresses. Imagine a week of airline-type kosher meals. They probably come from the same kitchens. But you won't starve. There are also totally-kosher cruises where the ship has been approved by the Rabbinical forces. *Shalom.*

Cruise ship waiters could teach the stereotypical Jewish mother something about guilt trips. If you dare to leave a morsel uneaten, the top-notch waiter assumes a look of confused dismay. "You did not like it?"

Hell, yes, I liked it, but I'm saving room for dessert. If you are not a plate-cleaner, make it clear to your waiter early on that you like to *taste* everything, just not *eat it all*. You will feel better and so will he. See the section on cruising without breaking your diet.

If you really don't like something—the *Crème of Crappie* soup was over-salted and you didn't care for the garnish of toasted fins—roll your eyes at the waiter and, when he shimmers over, say, with regret, "I just don't care for this." It will be off the table and he will be on his way to the kitchen for a replacement (or not, as you wish) at the speed of an Olympian in training.

At the same time, if you are extraordinarily pleased by a particular dish, seconds are usually available. The kitchen staff probably does not understand the idea of simply putting one piece of meat on a small plate and handing it to the waiter. Most likely, you will get an entirely new plate of food.

Just because the courses march relentlessly on, you don't have to have soup for the soup course. You can have a second appetizer, served with the others' soups. It's possible to mix-and-match your dinner, just as long as whatever you want is on the menu. If it happens to be an evening when you fancy both the *tiramisù* and the *crème brûlée* for dessert, ask for a second salad instead of an entrée.

Other Dining Venues

You always have a choice as to where you'll eat for breakfast and lunch. The casual restaurant, almost always a buffet, usually on the pool deck, caters to the hit-and-run crowd. The fare is rather steam-table predictable . . . particularly at breakfast. Scrambled eggs, pre-folded omelets, breakfast meats, semi-limp pancakes, fruits of all varieties (Kadota figs again!), dry cereals in their cunning little boxes, a hot cereal, yogurts, sweet rolls, bagels and, more often than not, a deli-style meat and cheese platter. On some cruise lines, there is smoked salmon—and more smoked salmon—especially if the bridge crew is Norwegian.

Most ships also offer a custom-cooked egg station where a chef wields his omelet pans with cheese, chopped vegetables and *élan*.

Come lunchtime, you may be taken by a hint of *déjà vu* when you notice that the salad dressings next to the green salad bar are the same ones that were served with dinner last night. There is always a green salad bar, followed by heartier salads based on pasta, rice and potatoes. Plenty of deli-type meats and cheeses invite you to make a sandwich while, further down the line, the "made dishes" stay warm. If you jump to the conclusion that these are last night's leftovers, you're close. They're not really leftovers, they're "planned-overs." If the kitchen is going to roast forty pork loins for dinner, why not roast forty-five so there's pork to go into a sauce with Oriental vegetables. They are very clever, these food designers.

If you look around, you'll probably find a cousin of this morning's omelet chef whipping up the pasta dish of the day. Almost at the end of the chow line, there's usually a carving station with a roast of something or other. Then, there's the final touch, desserts.

The fascination of U.S.-type cruisers with pizza is a mystery to non-citizens. One of the most frequently asked questions on the 'Net is,

"What about the pizza?" To some people, twenty-four-hour pizza is an important factor in choosing a cruise ship.

Around Noon, a grill area fires up every day on every cruise ship unless it's raining pitchforks or a gale-force wind has blown up. The available fare will be burger and dogs, dogs and burgers. The standard condiments are available for your Cheeseburger in Paradise and—um, did you want fries with that? It's not a highly creative lunch but if you don't feel like shuffling down a buffet line or just don't want to put shoes on, it's an option.

Some ships, particularly the mega-type with over 2,000 passengers, turn the casual restaurant into something a bit more upscale when the sun goes down. Generally, it's open seating so you can eat when you wish, the dress code is always casual, and the appetizers, soups and entrées are the same as those served in the Main Dining Room. The main difference is in the serving. Usually you serve yourself, buffet-style, everything but the entrée, which you order from the menu. The waiters will tell you what to do.

Some ships require reservations for this option; check the daily newspaper. This is not an option on all ships. If it's important to you—you refuse to dress up for formal night, for example—make sure you check the availability in advance.

> ⚠️ Some cruise lines extract a minimum charge for this option.

> 🍴 Not all evening transformations are equal. I never fail to be adventurous and see what's offered. On *Marco Polo,* we savored an Oriental dinner one night—complete with endless saki—and on another, an evening of French cuisine with fascinating wines. On NCL's *Norwegian Dream,* we were regulars at the line's signature alternative restaurant, "Le Bistro." On the Radisson *Diamond* we paid two visits to the high-energy "Don Vito's Trattoria," repeating a similar experience on that ship's fleetmate *Song of Flower.*
>
> The newer ships have raised the bar—and the tab—on alternative dining. Celebrity's Millennium-class ships all feature a dining

experience unparalleled at sea in the mainstream fleet. The surroundings are beyond elegant, harking back to the days of the great ocean liners. The service is impeccable, and the food is—in the common parlance—"to die for."

Try as I might, I can't find any commonalties among these experiences except for the small number of diners served with the corollary increase in quality and personal attention. Practically, the Main Dining Room does a fantastic job of serving upscale banquet food. The alternative restaurants are closer in ambience and quality to a landside restaurant.

A new wrinkle is dining at a variety of restaurants around the ship. Show up when you please; eat with whom you please. It all sounds very personal. It gets less personal when it seems like everyone else on the ship wants to eat where *you* want to eat, at the exact same moment *you* want to eat there.

Some people think it's a sin to pay extra for food when you've already paid for dinner in the Main Dining Room. Others can't wait for the special experience. Usually, reservations are required. Make them as soon as possible. Be aware that the dress code in specialty restaurants may not be the same as the rest of the ship's for the same evening. Coat and tie may be required for the gents.

Sometimes reservations are available, but the table for eight you might want to share with friends will only be available at 6:45 or 9:15. That doesn't do much if you wish to dine at 8:00 for eight. Getting personal in the personal choice area—a particular waiter or table for example—may be more frustrating than pleasurable.

Most cruisers don't explore room service any further than hanging their "coffee and" orders on the door before retiring for the night. The room service menu is in the nicely bound folder outlining the ship's services. The fare is usually simple—sandwiches, salads and desserts —but a fruit and cheese plate can be just the thing to tide you over before dinner. If you order a couple of sandwiches, they fit nicely in the Giant Tote Bag for a picnic ashore.

It used to be that only the luxury lines allowed guests to order from the regular dinner menu and have it served *en suite*. That's changing. Most now offer the opportunity to dine in your cabin, being served, course-by-course, by an attentive waiter or your cabin steward. Ask for a menu early in the day, peruse it, make your selections and prepare to enjoy. Tip well for this.

 While it sounds perfectly romantic—and completely delicious in every way—to eat in your underwear, take a close look at your cabin. Will the coffee table rise to dining table height or will you eat crouched over or sitting on the floor? How much room is there for your food?

Libations

Alcoholic beverages by the drink are expensive, on land or at sea. If you do indulge, it's not unlikely you'll be a little more likely to do so on a cruise vacation. After all, you're not driving.

Liquor is a profit center for ships just as it is for land-side restaurants. And, with the notable exception of one mainstream cruise line—though that may change—a standard fifteen-percent gratuity is added to every bar order, including soft drinks by the can and wine by the bottle in the Main Dining Room. This adds up rather quickly if you enjoy anything more than a single martini before dinner. What adds up even more quickly is kids and soda pop.

There are people who like beer. There are people who like a *lot* of beer, especially in hot weather. Beer at three or four dollars or more per can, plus fifteen-percent, gets pricey—as do soda pops at almost as much. I don't recommend you try to cart three or four cases of your favorite brewskis on board with a hand truck, but there are ways to self-supply. Buy enough cheap suitcases to hold your provisions. Cushion the contents with bubble wrap—top, bottom, and sides. Check your bags; do *not* attempt to carry on. Be warned, however. Some ships' policies are stricter than others and your spirits just might be confiscated.

Beer and sodas are rather disgusting when warm, so your cabin steward must be your new best friend. It's his job to figure out how to keep your supply cold. A discreet offering of cash will increase his interest in assisting and—once the beer is cold—make sure he knows that he's welcome to help himself.

An extremely efficient cooler can be constructed from an everyday shopping bag lined with a plastic trash bag. Fill with beer (or sodas) and add ice. Don't try this anywhere but in your cabin's shower. Remove before using the shower for its intended purpose. Don't forget foam can "cozies" . . . or you can buy them in the gift shop.

There's no hard-and-fast rule about bringing your own aboard. Each cruise line has its own policy. The policies range from, "If we find you bringing it on board, we'll confiscate it and give it back at the end of the cruise," to the far more liberal, "Please do not consume personal beverages in public areas." Almost all cruise lines allow you to bring a special bottle or two of wine or champagne aboard.

To further confuse things, some lines allow you to purchase spirits in the duty-free shop for immediate, on-board consumption, while others won't deliver your purchases until the last night out. This is definitely a "go figure" situation. Or, perhaps better, a "go find out" challenge.

We've never had a problem with tucking bottles into our suitcases, using clothes as breakage buffers. If you're truly paranoid, wrap each bottle in bubble wrap and seal inside a zip-top bag.

Of course, having bottles of liquor in your luggage (and for some reason, wheels or blocks of cheese) practically guarantees the TSA will search your bags at the airport. Check the TSA website before you pack.

As in many other things, discretion is the better part of valor. And why do you think almost every cabin features an ice bucket, glasses and cocktail napkins? Obviously, there's some sort of expectation that you might be carrying your own supply.

Why do you prefer the Late Seating to the Main Seating?

Basically, it gives us a longer day and we're accustomed to

eating on the late side at home. We also enjoy the time to relax before dinner after a day in port. If your stomach (or your kids') starts getting peckish in late afternoon, you're probably better off with Main Seating. Be warned, however, that main seating breakfasts come awfully early!

Do we really eat *all day?* What about the Midnight Buffet?

There's almost always food to be found somewhere on a cruise ship. Coffee and tea usually appear on a weather deck or in the casual restaurant at 6 a.m. Breakfast, or some form of it, is usually served until almost lunchtime. Casual lunch usually folds up in the mid-afternoon, not long before teatime which, in turn, isn't long before the first dinner seating. Some ships feature "happy hours" with appropriate snack foods—but the drinks aren't two-for-one.

If you're the late seating sort (we are) a cruise by the tea buffet yields delicacies that hit the spot with an in-cabin cocktail. A plate of little sandwiches, a plate of sweets, maybe fruit and cheese . . . whatever looks good. The stated policies usually say not to take food to cabins. This makes no sense because room service brings food to cabins all the time. There are no food police to stop you.

The every-night midnight buffet is almost a thing of the past in these calorie- and fat-conscious days. Instead, on some lines, hot snacks are passed in the public rooms around 11 p.m. and onward. However, there will be at least one big-deal midnight buffet—usually on the second formal night. Be prepared for a huge crush of people, all pushing to get to the food first. Most cruise lines offer a fifteen-minute grace period for folks who wish to photograph the opulence.

If this isn't enough food, there's always room service—on some cruise lines it operates twenty-four hours a day—complete with twenty-four hour pizza. It's a little weird to walk down a corridor and see pizza delivery boxes in the hallway when you know you're two hundred miles from the nearest land. My husband and I dissolved into a serious fit of giggles when we visualized a fast little boat or a helicopter with a lighted sign, "Pogo's Pizza Delivers." Hold the anchovies.

I don't think we could bring enough sodas to keep our kids supplied. What to do without breaking the budget?

There are almost always unlimited beverages available—usually iced tea, lemonade and fruit punch. Soda by the glass is usually included at dinner. Some enlightened cruise lines issue (sell) soda cards for unlimited fountain drinks.

Play fair with soda cards for kids. We once observed two families—four kids—that purchased a single soda card. The young lady to whom it was issued appeared at the bar approximately every nine minutes for another soda.

We've heard that cruise ship coffee is pretty awful. We are coffee snobs. Any ideas?

Of course. Remember, coffee for huge numbers of people is institutional-grade at best and just brewed will taste a lot better than the bottom of the pot. The one cruise line which had a reputation for perfectly terrible coffee finally found the problem and cured it.

There are two choices. Bring along individual coffee bags and order tea from room service and in the restaurants. Tea comes with hot water and tea bags on the side. Don't try to order hot water, it will only confuse the crew.

The second choice is to pack a small, four-cup coffee maker in your Creature Comfort Bag and bring along your own special blend. Don't forget the filters. You will probably need an extension cord unless you fancy making coffee during morning ablutions. The second approach does not work well in dining rooms.

You may find a specialty coffee café on your ship. Often the upscale coffees carry an additional charge. If the coffees contain liquor they will certainly cost extra.

What if we don't finish our bottle of wine at dinner? May we take it to our cabin?

Probably. Otherwise, your waiter will put it back in the cellar for you and bring it out at your request. The storage method is ideal if one person enjoys wine and the traveling partner abstains. It's also a good solution if one person prefers white and the other likes red.

We'd like to bring our own special wines along. Is that permitted? How does it work in the dining room?

This depends, largely, on the cruise line's policy. And there's always the delicious possibility that your travel agent or a friend will send a Bon Voyage bottle. Usually, personal wines are subject to a corkage fee, somewhere in the ten-dollar range.

Can we buy liquor in port and bring it on board?

Sure, if you're willing to pay local prices and be discreet as you carry it on. In some ports, if you purchase duty-free liquor, it will be delivered directly to the ship and held in bond until the last night out when it is delivered to your cabin. In others, if you can drag it away from the store, it's yours. Two popular ports, Bermuda and St. Thomas, take opposite tactics. Bermuda delivers to the ship and limits the amount of purchase per person. In St. Thomas, you can buy all you can carry.

However, if you are carrying, be prepared for an extra-officious crew member, possibly after a policy crack-down, to take custody of your purchases until the last night out.

Do cruise lines ever charge "extra" for food?

Some extract an extra charge for upscale ice cream bars, designer coffees, etc. And if you hit the caviar bar, you'll get hit. Almost always, specialty restaurants fall into this category.

What about special occasions? We're taking a cruise for a big birthday.

Your travel agent can make all the necessary arrangements for a cake to appear at your table, accompanied by a rather off-key rendition of the birthday song. (Same deal for anniversaries.) It's a good idea to check with the maitre d' to ensure that your wishes will be fulfilled.

CHAPTER NINE
CONSPICUOUS CONSUMPTION

In this chapter, we'll look at one of the ways you can part with money—and how to deal with money—on your all-inclusive cruise vacation. Other than tipping, there are two basic methods: shopping and gambling. Shopping definitely comes first.

A great American philosopher, Jimmy Buffett, once said that there are two kinds of Americans who leave our shores—tourists and travelers. A tourist wants to take America along on a trip. The traveler wants to experience something a bit different. What could be more American than taking along pictures of dead presidents—in the form of U.S. currency—in your wallet or purse?

Funny Money

If your destination is Totally Tourist—think the Caribbean or Mexican Riviera—you don't need to take anything but American money. When you reach ports where tourism isn't the number one pastime, you may need to exchange your money for the currency of your host country. Life on the other side of the Pond (Europe) has become a bit easier with the introduction of the Euro.

High on the strange level, I was able to purchase a beautiful linen dress in Tallin, Estonia for forty dollars, U.S. My husband, bored by waiting around for me, could not purchase a Coke at the McDonald's across the square because we hadn't scored any local currency. Not to be deterred, he found a food kiosk that did take U.S. money.

The ship's staff will happily exchange your U.S. money for local currency. The reason they are happy to do this is because they collect a fee for the service. They become even happier when you pay another service fee to put whatever you didn't spend back into U.S. currency—before they become ecstatic changing your new U.S. into the coin of the next realm. Again, the Euro has made life much easier in this respect.

Everyone's idea of walking-around money is different. We generally carry the equivalent of one hundred dollars per person, per day with another hundred dollar bill tucked deep into wallet or pocketbook in case of a true emergency.

You'll probably use a credit card for major purchases—but what about that Coke at McDonald's? So far, the only place we've visited that doesn't have McDonald's restaurants is Vietnam. We've never found a McDonald's outside the Caribbean that doesn't require local currency unless the local dollar is on a par with the U.S. dollar.

If you'll be taking public transportation, you'll have to pay in local legal tender.

 We once made a significant miscalculation on walking-around money. We were in St. Petersburg, Russia, freelancing. Blissed-out after several hours in the Hermitage (we paid the entry fees by credit card) we crossed the street and boarded the fast boat for Peterhof, a lavish summer palace—eighty rubles each. At the entry kiosk for the Palace, the martinet selling tickets wanted nothing to do with our U.S. dollars or our credit cards. A nice British couple offered to sell us the entry fee. A bus from another cruise line offered final salvation. . . we hitched a ride back to the pier with their official excursion group. The more exotic your port, and the further you go from tourist-related sites, the more likely you are to need local currency.

The best exchange rates—bar none—are found at American Express offices. With precious little time in many ports, the ship's trip probably won't include a stop at an American Express outpost. You may be better off biting the bullet and changing your money aboard ship. The truly thrifty can organize a cartel—maybe among their tablemates—and pay a single fee for changing several people's bucks and spreading the cost around. This assumes a flat fee regardless of the amount.

Travelers' cheques have a high "pain in the patoot" factor on cruise vacations. It takes time to buy them and time to change them into cash. Even if they're free, that's relative. Local currency on cruise ships is the American dollar. Change your travelers' cheques, then you get to pay the fee to change the U.S. dollars into real local—the local currency where you're getting off the ship. To some extent, travelers' cheques are a holdover from the days before universal acceptance of credit cards.

Assuming you don't get taken out by banditos on the way to the cruise ship, carrying sufficient cash is the easiest way to go. Once you board, your cash—except what you decide is indicated for an individual day, is in the safe along with your gambling and tip money—ready to go for the next day.

 Underwear offers a dandy way to stash cash. Ladies can put bills inside their bras (Wonder® or otherwise) and lots of the silk boxers sold these days feature condom pockets where folded bills may be carefully stored.

A major credit card company says, "Don't leave home without it." Actually, don't leave home without two different credit cards each—preferably zero-balance cards. You don't want to become the Purser's new best friend on debarkation day because you've maxed-out a card with purchases ashore or cash advances at the casino and Mr. Credit Card Company just says, "*No!*"

Why two? And why two different ones per person? If a pocket is picked or a purse stolen, you ought to cancel the cards immediately. The Purser's office is extremely helpful in such situations. You're probably not going to stop shopping, and you have to settle your on-board account, so the second person's cards come into play. If your traveling companion is not your spouse, each person should carry one of the other person's cards for a belt-and-suspenders level of security.

Credit card companies don't like to lose money when a card is stolen and huge balances are run up. The cardholder's liability is generally limited to only fifty dollars. Accounts with unusual activity—particularly unusual activity in a different area code—attract the attention of security folks. If security gets the information about an out-of-the-ordinary activity pattern, someone will call you to make sure you're the one who's been using the card. If you're on a cruise, you won't be answering the phone. The card company just might cancel the card and you'll be in for a rude surprise when you step up to the cashier to settle your purchases. For peace of mind, call your credit card companies and advise them that you will be traveling and making charges. And while you're at it, write down the international phone number for reporting a lost or stolen card.

El Shoppiando

Several years ago I invented the term *el shoppiando* to describe one of my favorite activities when I lived in San Juan in the early '70s. People who rarely or never engage in *el shoppiando* at home do so with a vengeance on vacations—cruises included. It may just be t-shirts for the kids and grandkids or it may be high-end jewelry, electronics or cameras.

Shopping falls into two classes—bargains and souvenirs. If one purchase can be both, you win. It's always fun to have a guest admire a *tchatchkai* and be able to answer, airily, "Oh, I found that in the greatest little shop in Cartagena—for only three dollars."

Folk arts and crafts are great souvenirs. Just make sure the piece is indigenous to the country. It's no fun to give a friend a little carved cat from your Caribbean vacation and notice, as she unwraps it, a sticker that says, "Made in China." The more tourist-oriented your destination, the less likely you are to grab a bargain.

It is your duty to shop; I assure you it will not be free. All mainstream cruise lines feature duty-free shops on board. That doesn't mean you won't have to pay import taxes when you return to the U.S. on the amount you spent—aboard ship or ashore—if it exceeds the amount designated by U.S. Customs. The oral tradition has it that your on-board purchases will be reported if they exceed a certain limit. Other unsubstantiated rumors include port vendors reporting large purchases.

Some ports—St. Thomas is the one that comes immediately

to mind for most people—are touted as "duty-free." To be sure, vice-related products (liquor and tobacco) are much cheaper than your own home port. But there hasn't been a true bargain in St. Thomas since Gerald Ford was President. I know. I keep looking. Recently, a Bottega Venetta bag was twenty dollars more than at the flagship store in New York.

If you want to cheat and buy more than your allowance of hooch, you probably won't get caught. Considering the off-shore discount of such pricey stuff such as liqueurs and cordials, it's quite probable that even if you pay the duty, you'll still come out ahead. If you can find a hometown purveyor of spirits who issues a catalog, take one along. Then you'll know for sure that fifteen dollars for the artichoke brandy is a good deal.

Bargains can usually be found in a product's country of origin. That's easy to understand, there are no shipping and no export / import costs. And there's the benefit of a refund of the Value Added Tax (VAT) in many European countries. But before you spring for that item, think how your bargain is going to find its way home. Filling out the forms for refund of the VAT can be an exercise in frustration.

 Once, in Stockholm, I came across some candleholders at a price that was considerably less than half of U.S. prices. I was so excited that I bought two dozen. I didn't stop to think that they weighed about a pound apiece. With today's more stringent regulations on baggage weight, my great bargain would have put me over the limit and I'd have been charged for the extra weight.

Another time, we visited an obscure suburb of Guadalajara, called Tlaquepaque. That's where artisans offer their works at wholesale to the proprietors of gift shops in true tourist areas. Jubilant at the purchase of several fat little clay women (*gorditas*) for a hundred dollars, I was over the moon to see the sister of one of them offered in Puerto Vallarta for two hundred dollars. I was less happy when my little fatties arrived in many, many, many pieces.

Not every port has a best bargain. As a rule, the closer any shopping outlet is to the pier, the higher the price. They see you coming, literally.

The number one rule for off-shore shopping is knowing what the same thing would cost at home. This applies to jewelry, probably more than anything else. If you're buying machined gold jewelry, ask to have it weighed. Semi-precious colored stones—tanzanite, aquamarine, garnet, topaz, kunzite, etc. are popular—and often overpriced—souvenir purchases. Know what a chunk of your stone of choice costs, then add (generously) a hundred dollars for the mounting and see if the dealer is in the ballpark. Don't get too excited if there are diamonds in the setting. Small diamonds cost almost more to mount than to buy.

I don't recommend purchasing the "Big Three and P"—sapphires, rubies and emeralds plus pearls—to say nothing of diamonds—anywhere but from a trusted jeweler stateside, unless you know what you're doing and your loupe is next to your credit cards. For jewelry—or any other significant purchase—use a credit card. If it turns out to be a good fake or appraises significantly lower than the purchase price, start screeching to the credit card company.

The people at the ubiquitous emerald stores will argue, but the most prized emeralds are not bright green nor are the best sapphires navy blue. The cost of these prized colors is out of range of most folks' pocketbooks. If you're buying a piece as a memento of your cruise, the important thing is that you like it and don't care whether or not you got a great deal. If you are thinking of the piece as an investment, you should be a lot more careful. Important stones should come with a certificate of authenticity.

Make sure you're comparison shopping for apples against apples, particularly with cameras, binoculars and electronics. Find a Sunday *New York Times* and rip out the 47th Street Photo ad or make a print-out of one of the many on-line stores. There's your standard of comparison. Out-of-date, remaindered items are not a bargain.

How to know when to bargain—as in haggle—and when not to? If you hadn't skipped the port lecture for the next stop, the Cruise Director probably would have told you the local customs. Ask the person sitting next to you on the deck.

If you ask a vendor, "How much?" and, in response to the first offer, you display your best look of confusion and minor disbelief and the price drops—he or she is open for bargaining. (This can be practiced in your bathroom mirror at home or aboard ship with a willing partner.)

If the "look" didn't do it, have your shopping partner say, "There was one like it for a lot less at that store around the corner." A response of, "Then buy it there!" definitely closes the bargaining door. The only way to save face in this scenario is for you to look at the shopping partner and announce, stoutly, "But I like this one better."

There's an unwritten law in some of the countries where bargaining rules that the beginning of negotiations means that a sale *will* take place. In other countries, walking away is just part of the game. The more expensive the item, the more important it is to be aware of local customs. If you waste a shopkeeper's time—particularly if you have accepted hospitality from him such as a cup of tea or a cold drink—and don't buy? Your name will be mud in that port before you're ever out of his establishment. There will be no bargains that day. Think angry shopowner-to-shopowner cell phone calls—whether in Tijuana or Istanbul.

 There is nothing worse to a confirmed practitioner of *el shoppiando* than going back to buy whatever it was that you were trying to find a better deal for only to discover that the store is closed for siesta and your ship's about to leave or that "it" was sold—probably to the person at the next table. I still mourn a beautiful silver necklace (shop closed) on Cozumel and a fabulous dress (sold) in Puerto Vallarta.

Sometimes the bargain finds you. I really didn't want those two sets of nesting baskets in Hanoi. How was I going to get them home? I just kept saying, "No." And I meant it. Finally, they were only two dollars, down from twenty. I bought them and dragged them halfway around the world. I forgot them on the limo on the trip home.

Credit for inventing the term "Moscow Theory of Shopping" and the associated *modus operandi* she recommends, belongs to one of my personal icons, Suzy Gershman, who has spent years shopping the world and writing about it. I want to be Suzy Gershman in my next life.

The "Moscow Theory" is a simple one: *See it, want it, buy it.* Of course, you have to really want it for the theory to kick in. It's your time you're wasting if you decide to cruise around to other stores to find a lower price—if you can even find the same thing.

The "Moscow Theory" applies particularly to cruisers on official shore excursions. You don't get much chance to shop around and escaping to shop on your own is seriously frowned upon in some of the more up-tight countries.

Uncle Sam Wants You(r Money)!

As you return from your vacation to the land of the (not) free and the home of the (sometimes) brave, you'll be asked to tell Uncle Sam, wearing his Customs Official outfit, just what you purchased when you were out of the country and how much you paid for it. It's not nice to fool either Mother Nature or Uncle Sam, but people do it, some more successfully than others.

In the process of interviewing a Customs Official at Kennedy Airport in New York, I learned the most fascinating—and backward—rule of all. If the person looks comfortably well-off and professes to have spent very little, a big red flag starts waving. Even if you really didn't spend anything (and we really didn't on a recent Caribbean cruise), say you did or you may have a new best friend in the Customs uniform looking through your lingerie.

He also shared some of the best-known dodges. Interestingly, they all involved jewelry and cameras and the compulsion of the would-be trickster to display them in the open. They are:

$ Pearls from the Far East: They are so perfect they almost look fake—except to the trained eye. They are usually strung quickly with shoddy knots and closed with a cheap clasp. *Gotcha!*

$ Other jewelry: There are rings or bracelets that would put a family of four over the limit in one fell swoop if declared. The jewelry looks filthy from intense applications of scouring pads without rinsing afterward. *Gotcha!*

$ The cameras: The latest, most expensive models keeping company with many fancy lenses draw attention. They look like they lost a blood feud fight with a riding lawnmower—dings, paint sanded off and a tacky old strap from a former camera are not good camouflage to the eagle eyes of the Customs guys. *Gotcha!*

$ Clothing: Customs officials probably know more about high fashion and other expensive goods than the editors of slick magazines. Some people think they can sneak by without paying duty if they are wearing a particular item. *Gotcha!*

$ It's a popular misconception that "worn" clothing is not subject to duty. What Customs wants to know is how much money you spent on things you are bringing into the country with you.

If you're over your limit by a few dollars, fudging can be tolerated. If you're w-a-y over, declare your stuff and haul out your credit card. After all, there are states whose sales taxes are almost equal to, if not more than, the Customs duty. The U.S. Government's computers are massive and mighty. If you get caught trying to gouge a few bucks in the Customs line, you have to wonder how closely the IRS is going to look at your next 1040.

A little honesty never hurt anyone. And the bureaucratic systems often work to your benefit. When you declare that you are four bottles over your limit for liquor, the response from the Customs official is likely to be a hand-wave, telling you to keep going. Does he really want to do the paperwork to collect seven dollars?

What if I run out of money?

That depends upon your definition of "run out." If you're out of cash, the casino cashier's cage will be happy to give you greenbacks for a fairly hefty charge against your credit card. Some cruise ships feature ATM machines. At least in our experience, by the time people line up to use them, they are empty. Helicopters do not fly in to replenish them.

If you run out of money in port, ATMs are almost everywhere. Some, however, require an international PIN. Make sure you know before you go.

> $ Growing up, I never really understood the term "mad money"—but my Mom always made sure I had some. I thought it was there for spending on something silly. . . not for finding my way home in time of crisis. Read that: I got mad at my date. Even though I'm an even-tempered person, I always travel with mad money—a crisp U.S. hundred or two, tucked behind my photo ID. My husband does the same. Remember those fast boats from Bermuda that can catch up to a departing cruise ship?

Can't I just write a check?

It's a good idea to have a check or two with you, but cash or credit cards rule travelers' commerce.

What if we have a pre-cruise hotel overseas? Where do we change our money?

If you arrive at your destination airport during daytime or early evening hours, there will probably be a change booth open and more than willing to zap you with a serious surcharge for changing your dollars.

If you're saving money with overnight flights, arranging your own transport to the hotel, or traveling on holidays—not ours, the holidays *there*—you may be out of luck. The best deal is what personal service bankers call "tip packs." They are usually available in multiples of twenty dollars in U.S. currency, changed into the Euros, pesos, drachmas, or rubles of your destination country. Ask for them ahead of time—two or more weeks. If the exchange rate is favorable and if you're a good customer of the bank, the transaction may be made without charge.

Once in your pre- (or post-) cruise country's hotel, the hotel's front desk is the most convenient place for exchanges, but the associated charge is high. You have to decide whether saving a dollar or two is worth the aggravation. Banks (and American Express offices) are always the best . . . but factor in the time lost standing in line.

How much money should I take, regardless of how I take it?

If you will be using a credit card for major purchases, on-board charges, or anything more than a cold beer or an inexpensive impulse item on shore, fifty dollars per day, per person, is a good starting point.

Taking a Chance

Craps float and so do blackjack, roulette, weird forms of poker (including video) and the ubiquitous slot machines. Cruising and casinos are almost synonymous. Then you've got your Bingo, your horse racing and your standard mileage pool. Opportunities to contribute to one of every cruise line's most important profit centers are almost everywhere.

At one time or another my husband and I have played all these games, with varying degrees of success. He can usually be counted on to win at least the tip money by posing as a five dollar James Bond at the blackjack tables. I reliably lose my stake to the slot machines with a few stunning exceptions—one was hitting a two-hundred-fifty dollar jackpot on *Marco Polo* the last night out as we steamed toward Sydney from Melbourne.

Did I say "last night out"? You bet. My encore performance was on *Westerdam,* a last night out, for over $2,000. *Right now* is the moment when you learn the real truth about shipboard slot machines. Make yourself an umbrella drink. Be seated.

Everybody—and that's almost everybody—*knows* and believes as gospel, that slot machines are "looser" the first part of a cruise and "tighter" as the cruise goes on. Everybody also knows that this is so passengers, made greedy by tales of big hits the first or second night out, will pour ever-increasing numbers of quarters into the one-armed bandits in hopes of hitting too. Right? Experienced cruisers, who *know the real truth* make their offerings to the gods of chance the first and second nights and stay away for the rest of the cruise. Right?

Wrong-o.

Did you ever stop to think just how such a thing could happen? Captain Stubing and Gopher creeping around in the dark of night with a device that looks like a roller skate key? Not likely.

Did you know that today's slot machines are nothing more (or less) than computers? Just like your personal computer, your personal slot machine has a chip called an EPROM—that means Electronically Programmable Read Only Memory. Read Only. That means that nobody—*but nobody*—can change what that chip tells the slot machine / computer without a whole lot of trouble. The entire computer (slot machine) has to be opened, the EPROM removed and reprogrammed or another put in its place.

Each machine is set to the cruise line's payout percentage when it leaves the factory. It doesn't change without replacement or reprogramming.

Here's the big secret: the cruise line can set the *real* jackpot, the one your chances of winning are about a bazillion to one. Standard jackpots are 10,000 to 25,000 coins. The worst news? Those reels with 7s and apples and cherries and whatever are not real. They're just there for the show. The computer already knows whether or not you've won before the reels start to spin.

Now that we've debunked that seagoing legend, what about the experience many of us have had? After pumping twenty dollars in quarters into a machine, we walk away in disgust. A sweet little old lady wearing a powder blue dress and sensible shoes drops in a few quarters. All the bells and whistles go off, stopping us in our tracks. Granny hit the jackpot. If only we'd pulled the handle *one more time*. Give it up; it makes no difference at all.

New sets of numbers are constantly being generated in a random fashion by the machine's infernal internal computer. Your "hit" is determined by the exact second (or, more likely, nanosecond) you push the button or pull the handle, not by the number of cumulative plays on that machine.

If you hit a really big jackpot on the slots, the bells and whistles do not go off. A signal is sent to the cashier's cage and the only indication that you've made a big hit is the flashing light on the top of the machine. On my only big hit, I thought the machine was broken because it wouldn't take any more quarters.

We don't need anyone to teach us how to pull the handle or push the button. The other games afloat are a bit more challenging to the novice.

If a ship has only one table game, it's blackjack. The concept is simple: Whoever—you or the dealer—is closest to twenty-one without going over, wins. Arguably, blackjack (and its wealthy cousin baccarat) is the only casino game where intelligence, experience and skill come into play. Entire books have been written on "How To Win At Blackjack" and there are several outstanding computer games to help you learn the necessary skills. Most cruise lines provide gaming guides for passengers. The casino staff is happy to teach you the ins and outs of table games during an at-sea day—*before* you hit the tables in the evening.

Just as each table has a minimum—the least expensive tend to be five dollars—it has a maximum. There's a good reason for this. Anyone with a passing knowledge of statistics knows that, sooner or later, you're going to win. So, if you double your bet each time you *lose*, you'll at least stay even when the winning hand appears. Doubling losses works only five times at blackjack tables. If you lose the sixth hand, you're done.

The term "high roller" came, originally, from the craps tables but these days it means anyone with a significant amount of money to gamble. True high rollers are rare on cruise ships; they don't like to consort with the amateurs. "Medium rollers" are more frequently observed. Probably only the casino staff will know who the rollers are—they come aboard with letters of credit from land-based casinos. A $20,000 letter of credit is medium. $50,000 is high.

Most of us won't share table space with serious players, but if one happens along, there's a dramatic change in the aura surrounding the table. The dealer, cheerful and helpful to the honeymoon couple at the end of the table up 'til now, turns serious. Your five-dollar ante suddenly looks paltry compared to the fellow with the diamond pinky ring playing two hands at fifty or a hundred dollars each. Remember, you're playing against the dealer just as the roller is. Concentrate.

Roulette may be the most benign casino game ever invented. With any luck at all, placing only the most conservative bets, you can while away two or three hours at the wheel of fortune without winning much or losing everything. There are two fifty-fifty bets available—red or black, odd or even, excluding the "greens," zero and double zero, which makes the odds more like forty-seven / fifty-three in favor of the house.

Craps is fast-paced and, at best, confusing to the uninitiated. This may be why the house enjoys the *least* advantage of any game. In simplest terms, when a *new shooter* comes out by taking the dice, he or she rolls the dice to determine the *point* that must be made on a subsequent roll. Everyone else pressing around the table bets on the likelihood of the roller hitting the point on the next toss. Or the toss after that—or after that.

You're on your own putting chips down where you think you want them to be; there's no middleman in craps. The only way most people can tell how they're doing at craps is watching the croupier deal with their stacks of chips. If he takes them away, you lost. If he shoves another stack over, you won. You have just learned everything you need to know about craps. It's all about statistics. No skill required.

Nowhere else are the odds more in favor of the house (cruise line) than in the ever-proliferating forms of stud poker. This isn't sitting around, drinking a beer, smoking a cigar, bluffing your buddies, poker. It's serious (and expensive) business. You—and everyone else at the table—are playing against the dealer. The rules are bizarre and vary from cruise line to cruise line, game to game. If you happen to win, it's a big win. Otherwise, it's the ocean-going version of pouring money down a rat hole. "Let it Ride" is a fascinating method of extracting even more money from players under the guise of, "Hey, this is so easy even I can play it."

The non-casino games—Jackpot Bingo, horse racing, and the mileage pool—are, say casino managers, for entertainment only.

Arguably, it's easy to be entertained by winning a few thousand dollars playing Jackpot Bingo on the final night of the cruise. Again, it's pure chance.

The one place where you think you *might* be able to score is the mileage pool. If you're contemplating taking a laptop computer and a GPS system, forget it. My husband and one of his buddies tried it. They knew, within seven feet, exactly where in the middle of the ocean we were and, through a few quick mathematical calculations, *knew* exactly how far the ship had traveled. They put some serious money into the pool, as did the bikini-clad babes watching the distinguished looking gentlemen figure it out. Did they win? No.

That night at dinner, I braced the Master of the Vessel about this problem. "Ah, Madame. Somebody on the bridge makes up the number. It is usually close."

Our gambling experiences range from the two blackjack tables and seven slot machines aboard Radisson's *Song of Flower* to the megaships where you'd swear you were in Atlantic City if the deck wasn't rolling. Our luck is about the same in either situation. The only place where luck doesn't play a huge factor? Skilled blackjack players are the only ones with any advantage.

One of the big differences between casinos afloat and those ashore is the attitude of the dealers, croupiers and other casino employees. Years back, on-board casinos were usually concessions. Today, most cruise lines staff the casinos with their own employees. Ashore, dealers and croupiers (to say nothing of pit bosses that remind us of pit bulls) are not always the heart and soul of charm. Instead, they're all business—Big Business. At sea, the casino employees are as important to the cruise experience as the cruise director, the purser's staff or anyone else passengers meet along the way. The difference? On land, the destination is a casino or casinos with the express purpose of the trip being *gambling*. On a cruise ship, gambling is just one of many entertainments.

According to one cruise line's Vice President for casino operations, "Casinos have to match other customer services and facilities, then try just a little bit harder. Almost everything else aboard is free!"

A few truths about gambling at sea; most learned the hard way:

$ You'll almost always walk through the casino on your way to anywhere else. This is called marketing.

$ Once you're aboard the ship, separate the cash you'll need for tips on the final night, put it in an envelope, and stash it in the safe.

$ Know what you can afford to lose and chalk it up to "entertainment."

$ The biggest mistake you can make is pouring your (rare) winnings straight back into the casino's coffers. Wouldn't you rather have that Coogi sweater from Australia, a Lalique figurine or a Colombian emerald instead of another few minutes at a table or a machine?

$ The fastest and best way to rid yourself of your gambling stake is seating yourself in front of a video poker or blackjack machine. This won't hurt, will it?

$ *Always, always, always* wash your hands when you leave the casino. There's a reason for calling it "filthy lucre." It is. This is especially true for those who play the slots and handle coinage rather than chips.

$ Know that every time you hit your sign and sail card for the max ($1,000 or $1500 per day on most cruise lines) you're probably going to be looking at that bill for a long time to come as well as possibly paying a percentage—usually three percent—of your funds as a handling fee. And, in the worst of worlds, you may max-out your card completely. This is a way to become the Purser's new best friend at debarkation when your credit card company says "No" to your on-board charges.

 Some people figure that the Frequent Flyer miles they get from taking cash against a credit card—assuming the issuing bank offers Frequent Flyer miles—is worth it. It's not fun when they max-out their credit cards. According to the experts, this money is treated as a charge, not a cash advance

Did you ever want to know why, when you hit a jackpot, the first hundred or so coins spew out of the machine and the balance is paid by the staff? It's to keep a stash of coins in the machine for the next victims. Casino management wishes it could be different; winners who've just been handed the big bucks tend to leave the casino rather than playing on.

Whatever your gambling pleasure, get ready to hear the cha-ching of slot machines as soon as your ship clears U.S. coastal waters or leaves a foreign port. Chips ahoy!

Artful Dodger

The ubiquitous art auctions on board are another way to part with significant money. Just as in buying off-shore jewelry, *know* what you are buying.

If you see a piece that you just have to have, it's not inappropriate to enter into private negotiations with the art auction person. The worst than can happen is that the person will say, "No."

Also, there is often a reserve price on each piece. If nobody bids above the reserve, it will be removed from the auction.

Chapter Ten
To Your Good Health

We're not given a free pass from health problems for our vacations on land or sea. Life, with all its associated perils, happens on ships. On one of today's mega-ships with 3,000 passengers and, maybe, 2,000 in crew, somebody is going to get a cold or the flu. Somebody may have a heart attack. Somebody's going to break a tooth or have a dental crown fall off. Another person may trip over his or her own shoelaces or a life vest strap and break an arm. Another, just getting used to new bifocals, may miss a step in port and suffer abrasions or a broken bone. The very brave, renting scooters in port, may not quite understand how to operate them safely and wipe out with the associated injuries. Those who rent cars may forget that margaritas and driving don't mix, regardless of whether it's you or the guy in the other rent-a-Jeep. And, maybe, somebody will die.

The best way to put this into perspective is to consider a small town of 5,000 people. Life happens. It doesn't stop because you are on a cruise ship.

The best defense is a good offense.

The first thing to remember is that you are not just around the corner from your local hospital or an emergency care unit that is up to the standards you expect. You may be hours or days from skilled medical care. There is no way to call 911 at sea and expect the paramedics to show up. The second thing to remember is that "skilled medical care" can mean something *very different* on remote islands or third-world countries—and that you may not speak the language.

To Insure or Not

High on the list of important things to do is purchasing insurance for your cruise. It comes in two types: trip cancellation insurance and medical care when out of the country. Trip insurance is generally a package deal covering both perils. Cruise lines are willing to sell you a policy, but far better and broader coverage is usually available from third-party carriers.

"Going naked," as it's called in the insurance industry—without coverage—isn't too huge a risk so far as your cruise fare and airfare are concerned. Losing the trip money is a bite, but not a big one. The medical part is where you want to be as covered as possible.

Good trip cancellation policies include such arcane benefits as being able to receive a refund if called for jury duty, you get fired from your job or your home is burglarized within ten days of departure. They also include bail bond—something few of us consider as a necessity, but it's a nice touch. It's more likely that you or a traveling companion will (God forbid) fall ill before the cruise and be unable to go. Cancellation insurance also covers family emergencies such as death in the family.

Should you or a companion (Heaven forefend) fall ill on the cruise, this is where the medical part really kicks in. A visit to local medical providers is covered, with no deductible and no co-pay. If you're too sick to continue the voyage, a *per diem* is set for your companion to stay in the city where you are and your medical bills will be paid. If you're really sick and need medical evacuation, in most cases, it's covered. Check with your insurance agent for limitations. Evacuation Stateside on your own nickel can cost up to $20,000—if not more—and would take a large gouge out of your future cruising budget. If you become past sick and need to be returned home at less than room temperature (this is called "repatriation of remains") that's included, too.

Each policy is different and this is a time to read the fine print and make comparisons. Then write the check.

The second most important thing you can do is be *totally straight* with your travel agent about any health problems you may have. After many cruises, I may not have seen it all, but I've seen a lot of it.

 There was the gentleman who, three weeks post-surgical from a double knee replacement, continued with his plans for a fifteen hour flight from Los Angeles to the Antipodes—meaning in old Colonial parlance, Australia and New Zealand. He probably was looking forward to the relaxation, but didn't consider what the pressurization of the aircraft was going to do to his un-healed wounds. While he was comfortably asleep in a seat across the aisle from me and I was doing my best to join him in the arms of Morpheus, I noticed something strange—spreading, dark stains on his khaki pants. His wounds had split.

As a former flight attendant, I knew this spelled trouble and made my way to the aft buffet where the crew was taking a breather after serving dinner, cleaning up and lowering the lights so folks might sleep.

The flight was completely full; there was nowhere to put the gentleman to raise his legs. We managed to assemble a few pairs of pantyhose from ladies' carry-ons and build pressure bandages for him. He was somewhat grouchy about being awakened for "no reason," but once he'd seen the bleeding he grudgingly acquiesced to first-aid measures.

But it got worse. His wife, who was to be his wheelchair "pusher" on the cruise, apparently didn't hear the warning that, on this particular ship, the seals for the watertight doors were *above* the floor level. She managed to trip over one and broke her arm. Most passengers soon learned their son was a lawyer.

On another cruise, a lady just getting used to bifocals tripped over a curb, breaking one leg and both arms. She was on an official shore excursion, so was immediately returned to the ship. From there, she was taken to a shore-side hospital to determine her injuries and to have her limbs put in casts. Then she was put in sick bay with plenty of drugs.

Her husband was a man of many minds. He wanted to know why they couldn't just fly home *now*? The answer was that cabin pressurization in a plane would have put his wife in exquisite pain until the swelling from newly-casted injuries went down. Then he wanted to know why the cruise line couldn't fly *her* home so he could continue his cruise? And *how much* would it cost? Nice guy. Nice try.

Also, make sure that your emergency contact on your documents is *really* the person you want to have called—and that person(s) will be available twenty-four / seven.

> If it were not so pathetic, this would be funny. A fellow who took off for a cruise with a lady friend—telling his wife something entirely different—suffered a mild heart attack at the Tivoli Gardens in Copenhagen. He was treated at the hospital and released to fly home, but his "emergency contact" was more than a little surprised to find out that her husband was in Denmark rather than Dallas.

Think smart

If you are not accustomed to walking two or four or ten miles a day, don't sign up for high-impact shore excursions, regardless of how attractive they sound. If you've never learned to swim or float, make sure that water adventures are right for you.

Another thing to consider—and consider seriously—is if you are life-dependent upon mechanical devices. On one cruise, a passenger who (or whose travel agent) hadn't bothered to check on whether the person's portable dialysis machine was compatible with the ship's current got an undreamed-of cruise—from New York Harbor back to dry land, within an hour of sailing. The "ship" for this excursion was a cage dropped from a Coast Guard helicopter. The evacuee's travel companion had no choice but to endure two long days at sea until it was possible to fly back to New York from Bermuda.

Stupidity is not covered by insurance.

Some folks with pulmonary (lung) problems require a constant flow of oxygen. Others can make do with being hooked up to oxygen assistance for a number of hours each day, usually overnight. The home versions of oxygen tanks and other oxygen-assisted devices are not too ship-friendly. Fortunately, there are (expensive) services, which will deliver portable devices to cruise ships. If you need such machines, don't dilly-dally at boarding. Make sure your machine works, works properly, and that you have sufficient supplies for even the longest imaginable time away from a port. Also, tell your cabin attendant *not* to lay a finger or a dust cloth on your portable machine.

Plan Ahead

Many health-related and quality of life issues are so everyday, so commonplace, that it's easy to forget about them totally. Hearing aid batteries don't last forever and it's easy to forget to pack them. A hearing aid from your home country may use completely different batteries than those available somewhere else. Replace your batteries before you leave and take along twice as many as you think you will need.

It's a dog-eat-dog world and some of the smallest problems—once they affect your feet—can ruin a day or a cruise. New shoes can raise painful blisters. Sweaty feet can bring on a case of athlete's foot faster than mushrooms come up after a Spring rain. Or what if you get a mildly sprained ankle? Ouch! Remember the Fang and Claw bag? Moleskin *before* a blister arises is a world-class idea. Afterwards, it still works. Don't even think about the Band-Aid approach. A small can of foot powder is worth its weight in gold in fighting athlete's foot. And don't forget an elastic bandage of the "Ace" variety for those sprains and strains.

Tacky though it may sound, plain old white cotton socks may be your feet's best friends. And, even tackier, your well-worn-in shoes are far more foot-friendly than something brand new. Just put the smelly things in a zip-top bag before packing.

I'm scared of being seasick. What's the best remedy?

It's hard to prove a negative . . . many people swear by one potion or remedy because they've never suffered the tortures of *mal de mer*. If you have, it's an experience not to be repeated.

There are over-the-counter remedies such as Dramamine, Dramamine II and Bonine. Dramamine II and Bonine promise that they're non-drowsy, but they can provide the sensitive with a sound afternoon nap. In heavy weather, the Purser's Office or the ship's medical staff will probably be handing out a generic medicine upon request.

"The Patch," worn behind one ear, uses the drug Scopalamine.

"Scope" was used in years past to dope up ladies in labor. It still hurt, they just didn't remember. If it doesn't work, you'll remember.

"Sea Bands" are stretchy, bracelet-like devices that work on the principle of acupressure. They look strange with cocktail dresses. There's also a relatively new product running around that looks like a watch. It sends small electrical shocks—and it's not cheap.

The natural, non-intrusive, remedy of choice is ginger capsules, available at your local health food store, or plain crystallized ginger from the spice department of your favorite grocery store. Some people take along a couple of bags of gingersnap cookies.

None of these will do much good if you're already ill. At the first sign of seasickness—usually a non-specific, minor sinus-type headache—take your medicine and get yourself to a weather deck. The worst thing you can do is take to your bunk, contemplating the pitch and roll of the ship and your stomach in unison.

If your stomach goes a bit south, avail yourself of a time-tested remedy. Ask the bartender for a glass of club soda and his little bottle of Angostura Bitters. Shake the Bitters lustily into the soda (about ten shakes), mix and consume. A slice of lime is allowed for the sporty.

If the absolute worst happens, guard against dehydration. Eating apples provides plenty of fluid and they tend to stay down better than plain liquids. Call room service for some saltine crackers. If you're in serious "hurl" mode, apple juice is the sip of choice. Stay away from the citrus. Ships' doctors are prepared to give anti-nausea injections for extreme cases.

What's the best cabin location on a ship so I don't get seasick?

The least motion is amidships, as low as possible. Modern ships are equipped with massive stabilization systems so the motion of the ocean is, usually, imperceptible. But the best place is still in the open air.

What kind of medical services can I expect to find on my ship?

For the most part, limited.

There are no dentists on cruise ships, except as passengers. Taking a dental anesthetic along in case of a toothache is a good plan. If you lose a crown, "glue" it back on with toothpaste.

Ships' hospitals are prepared to deal with minor cuts, sprains, burns and simple broken bones. They can handle first-line aid for heart attacks, strokes, and more serious injuries, but the passenger will probably be hospitalized at the next port of call and med-evaced home.

This brings us back to that one word: insurance. The cost of a flight home after hospitalization could keep you cruising for the rest of your natural life. Don't leave home without it. The cost is minimal; the security level is maximum.

OK, Doc. Anything else I should take along, health-wise?

Yes. Pack over-the-counter preparations for the lower GI tract in both "Go" and "No-Go" types. You don't want to spend any part of your cruise hanging around in the head with that Montezuma guy—also known as "the runs." Diarrhea left unchecked can not only ruin your vacation, but lead to more serious problems.

Many cruisers, particularly women, suffer from the opposite problem. While not fatal, constipation can really put a cramp in your vacation. It may be the rich food, not drinking as much water as usual, or just the unfamiliar surroundings. But Mrs. Montezuma gets her revenge, too. The problem compounds—who wants to guess when a laxative is going to hit?

The best defense is a good offense. Right after boarding, drink two or three glasses of water, eat an apple and take a mild laxative just to get things back on schedule after a hectic travel day.

Don't forget an anti-acid preparation in case the caviar hits you wrong, an antibiotic ointment in case of a cut, a cold / allergy remedy, and a few Band-Aids. If you are prone to hemorrhoids, toss in your favorite "preparation" and don't hesitate to use it.

Is it really OK to drink the water?

The standards for potable (drinkable) water aboard ships are probably far more stringent than your local water company's. Bottled "designer" water is free on six-star ships, part of the cabin complement on mid-range ships (usually for a charge) and non-existent on some other lines. Bring your own water with you and re-fill the bottle from the bathroom tap. You may want to squeeze a slice of lemon or lime into the drinking water just for taste.

Strangely, if you don't drink enough water, you'll tend to retain water to take care of what you haven't had. Fingers and feet will swell. A mild diuretic is a good addition to the medical bag. Failing that, eat three cucumbers—although a pill is preferable. Use the cucumbers for puffy eyelids.

Anything else for the ladies?

Well, yes. If you're "of a certain age" and the Period Fairy hasn't paid one of her regular visits for a while, be prepared and pack some feminine hygiene products. You really don't want to send your husband to the disco at midnight to ask a hard-partying young lady, "Excuse, me Miss, but you wouldn't happen to have . . . ."

What if I drink too much and feel rotten the next day?

It's happened to lots of us. Before going to bed, take two aspirin, ibuprofen, etc. and drink two huge glasses of water. If you've *really* overindulged, put a glass filled with ice cubes next to your bed. By the time you wake up thirsty, it will be cold water. Put two more of those pain-relievers next to the ice cubes / water.

A cruise is *not* the time to worry about whether or not you should sign up for a Twelve-Step program. Call the dog and ask for some hair. Many people swear by the Bloody Mary, but the Salty Dog is king: Grapefruit juice, either gin or vodka, with the glass rimmed with salt. My personal creation, "Beach Juice," is good for almost any occasion and doesn't require alcohol: half-and-half orange juice and tonic water with a wedge of lime. It's refreshing, replaces lost electrolytes, and can be beefed up with Beefeater's gin, vodka, or rum.

OK. I am really sick. It's the flu of the world. What now?

Take comfort. There's not a much better place in the world to be ill than on a cruise ship. Where else can you release your partner from taking care of you, have someone changing your bed each day (or more often if you ask), and nobody has to clean the bathroom. OK, it's not fun. But, you also have a twenty-four hour supply of Jell-O, dry toast and hot tea. The doctor is just a holler away.

Once you start to feel better, stay with what physicians call "white foods" such as rice, mashed potatoes and roasted chicken. Avoid fried foods, richly sauced foods, weird combinations of mystery foods and cruciferous vegetables such as broccoli, cauliflower, and cabbage. Red meat is better on someone else's plate.

What about *awfully* sick—like dead?

That happens, too. Unless the dear departed departs in the view of many, it's usually not advertised. Ships' doctors are not morticians and cruise lines don't like to talk too much about what happens to the ex-passengers.

Deaths at sea are handled with extreme discretion, both out of respect for the deceased and his or her family and the associated public relations issues. Bodies are no longer tossed overboard. Instead, they are taken to the ship's morgue area—it's in the service area of the ship.

The first concern, though the family's grief and loss must be considered, is the safety of other passengers, particularly for health reasons. As quickly as possible, the body is zipped into a sealed body bag to prevent the spread of any possible illness among the passenger complement. The body cannot be embalmed at sea, and must be off-loaded at the next port. The sealed bag is refrigerated.

The essential tasks will be handled and expedited by the Purser's staff, under the direction of the Hotel Manager. The first step is to contact the American (or another country, if the person is not a U.S. citizen) Consulate in the next port of call to make arrangements to remove the body. A local funeral director will be engaged to oversee the removal of the remains. Families have very little, if any, choice in this.

The body will be removed, discreetly, from the ship before it is cleared. Usually, the body bag will be further enclosed in a sealed metal box, often called a "Ziegler case" and transported to the local funeral director for embalming.

Once embalmed, the body will be flown home, wherever that might be, to be collected by the hometown funeral director at the closest airport. This can be an extremely expensive process, which might make people ask the question of whether it might not be better to cremate the departed one, saving charges for shipping weight. Most good insurance policies cover these unexpected happenings.

Cremation may not be possible. It might also require residency requirements depending upon the port of call. It's hard to think logically in time of grief. If there is a comfort, it's knowing that the ship's staff, in a caring and discreet manner, will do everything that's possible to make the final disembarkation as comfortable as possible for those who are left behind.

CHAPTER ELEVEN
GOOD MANNERS AFLOAT & CAREFUL CONSIDERATIONS

Here's where we collected all the good questions that deserve good answers and didn't fit anywhere else.

I'm a smoker and I don't like to give offense to non-smokers. Are there special rules for ships?

There are some (very few) non-smoking ships, but you probably won't be taking one. Usually, smoking is permitted on one side of the ship and not on the other. Look for the ashtrays. Some six-star liners have a smoking area in the dining room, but most ships don't. You can always sneak out of the dining room between courses if you really must smoke.

For safety reasons, don't wander around holding a lighted cigarette and whatever you do, don't toss cigarettes overboard. They might end up on a lower deck.

Some newer ships feature "cigar bars" but, for the most part, pipe and cigar smoking is kept to the weather decks. You might want to stock up on smoking materials before leaving port to make sure that you'll have your favorite brand in sufficient quantity.

Warning: Don't count on hitting a duty-free shop. Some keep capricious hours and don't have a wide selection when they *are* open.

I don't smoke . . . can't stand it. But what if someone I really want to talk with smokes?

Ask if the person wouldn't mind sitting in a no-smoking area for a chat. I credit a friend with the best line I've ever heard. "I just quit smoking and I'm afraid if I'm anywhere near smoking I may have to kill someone and steal their cigarettes."

Is there a graceful way to disengage from someone I really don't want to spend time with? We were "adopted" by a person on our last cruise and I couldn't figure out what to do.

Short of being rude or tossing the person overboard, consider this to be a test of your social skills. I don't know anyone who would say, "Yes, I do mind," if asked, "Do you mind if I join you?" Of course you'll hate giving up your prized lounge chair but, "Oh, I was just leaving," is about the best you can do. Never mind if you just got there. Be wary of open-ended questions from your less-than-favorite people. "What are you doing tonight?" is a good example. In response to a specific invitation—say, for cocktails—an absent spouse is useful. "I'll need to check with Hector to see if he's made any plans." Unfortunately, the adoptive type doesn't take hints unless they're wrapped around cinder blocks.

We're so lucky. We're always in a cabin next door to a couple who fight (or love) loud and long late at night. Or, worse, they have a screaming child. By day, they're delightful people, but I like to sleep.

This is a touchy one. In my own experience, we were kept awake all night during a rough crossing of the Tasmin Sea by the folks next door. They kept slamming dresser drawers. In retaliation, I slammed a few back at them since I was awake anyway. I was mortified to see them coming out of their cabin the next morning—two delightful ladies I'd played bridge with several times. As I was working up to my best blush, one lady inquired, "It sounds like you were having the same trouble with those self-opening drawers that we were." Fortunately, the ship's carpentry staff solved that problem.

In the case of loud or lusty adults, mention the problem to the Purser. They won't know if it was you, the cabin steward, or the people on the other side when they are approached and asked to keep it down.

Also speak with the Purser about the crying child. You can't stop the child from crying, but there may be another cabin available.

Failing that, purchase earplugs at your next port stop if you didn't bring them with you.

Omigosh! We've been invited to dine with "The Master." What do we do?

You probably found the invitation to dine with the Captain under your door or on your bed. It says "r.s.v.p." *Respondez* immediately (you will probably say yes). The most elegant way is to write a small note of acceptance on the ship's stationery and deliver it to the front desk, but a phone call to the number on the invitation works as well. If you must decline, do so even more quickly.

> *Mr. And Mrs. Croozier (Cabin 1053) are delighted to accept the Captain's invitation for dinner this evening at eight-thirty.*

Do not be late. You'll be told where to gather—usually in a lounge. The Captain probably won't be there, especially on the first formal night, because he's doing his thing in the show room. The Social Hostess or a staff officer will meet you, make sure you have an appropriate libation, and introduce you to the other favored few.

After drinks, you'll be led to the Captain's table, which is always in a prominent spot. Don't trip over your hem; the whole dining room is watching the grand procession. There are always place cards, so don't worry about where to sit.

There will be plenty of wine, if you so choose. The worst gaffe you can commit is to ask for another cocktail.

The Captain leads the dinner chat, usually beginning by speaking with the lady on his right. When the first course arrives, the table "turns" and the Captain speaks with the lady on his left. The rest of the table follows the same pattern with each subsequent course. With an amiable group, the formalities are usually suspended by the time dessert is served.

A ship's photographer will come around to take a photo that you'll treasure for the rest of your life. Usually, the photo will show up in your cabin, compliments of The Master.

Write a thank-you note.

But my husband didn't bring a tux. Can we still join the Captain?

Of course. So long as he did bring a dark suit or, at the very least, a jacket and a tie. Many ships have a rent-a-tux facility.

We met a lovely couple on our last cruise and exchanged addresses. They invited us to visit "any time"—now we find we'll be near them on an upcoming trip. What to do?

Unless you became wildly fast friends, don't assume that the invitation includes a free room at their residence. A note (or e-mail) telling them that you'll be in the area on certain dates and would love to see them again is the appropriate opening volley. Tell them where you will be staying or ask for a rooming recommendation. You want to take them to dinner. Let them set the boundaries.

At the same time, be a little bit careful about "shipboard romances" on your end when you extend an invitation. The folks who were the life of the party on board may be quite different on dry land.

What about hurricanes?

Hurricanes tend to occur in the August-November time frame, though the official season begins in June. A cruise in Hurricane Alley during these months always carries a risk. But the risk isn't that you'll be caught in one. You might leave port a day early to get out of the way, you might skip a port entirely, or you might think you're going to Hamilton (Bermuda) and end up in Halifax (Nova Scotia).

Rest assured that the Captain and the decision-makers at the cruise line are not going to put their expensive ship and your precious well-being in harm's way. Also take comfort in the fact that the slowest cruise ship can easily outrun one of Mother Nature's temper tantrums.

It's also possible that a hurricane makes a visit to your destination before your cruise. If there's been significant damage, the cruise line will probably decide to skip the port entirely or substitute another.

**Can I call home from the ship? Can I check with
my office? What about faxes? Or the Internet?**

Yes, yes, yes and maybe.

Be warned. Making a phone call or sending a fax is very expensive. Not long ago, traveling with a friend, I sent a one-page fax to my husband in which I professed to be having a miserable time. The cost was over thirty dollars. *Then* I was miserable.

With the advent of Internet cafés afloat, we're seeing the shipboard communications revolution, but the connections are still very pricey. You'll do better with the Internet cafés in many port cities. Ask your waiter or cabin steward where to find the ones on land. They know.

What if someone needs to call me?

Check your travel documents when they arrive. There will be instructions on how to reach the ship either by telephone of fax.

**What does it mean when the brochure says that
we will tender to a private island?**

Assuming you know what a private island is, it means that you are taken off the ship into a boat—usually one of the ship's lifeboats, and then taken ashore. That boat is called a *tender*. A platform is rigged and you step—with the assistance of crew—from the platform aboard the tender.

The reason for tendering is that the ship's keel (the part under water) is simply too deep to come into shore.

But *be careful*. That leap from platform to tender isn't for the lame, the halt or the inebriated. Wear sensible shoes—preferably with "stick to the deck" soles. If you're lugging a lot of parcels on the way back, stare down the crew assistants and hand them the parcels *first* before you leap lithely from the tender. You want both hands available for the helpful crew members to get you transferred safely.

When you're on the tender, *sit down*. Tenders are not usually the smoothest rides in the world. They're slow and—especially in the Caribbean—it can be hot inside and the sun can be brutal up top. If you have *any* tendency toward seasickness, this is the time to hit the anti-nausea meds.

That doesn't sound like too much fun. What happens if there are a lot of waves?

If there are a lot of waves, you won't be tendering. It's too dangerous. The Captain decides on tendering operations and, not infrequently, private islands are skipped because of weather and the associated safety factors.

What happens if someone falls overboard?

It's unlikely that anyone will fall overboard by accident. Ships are well-designed to make sure that anyone but a few professional basketball players will have their centers of gravity below the rails on a weather deck or the rails in balcony cabins. It takes work (and desire) to go overboard.

If a "Man Overboard" alert is sounded to the bridge, the ship will slow down and execute a turn that, first, will get the propellers as far away as possible from the person reported to be in the water. The most basic maneuver is called a "Williamson Turn" which looks like a backward question mark and should return the ship to the place where the Man Overboard was first reported. The instructions for the Williamson Turn are posted on every bridge. Thankfully, they are rarely used.

I've heard a lot about shipboard "romances" with crew members. Are the stories really true?

Maybe the only true part is that the romances only last for the length of the cruise. I have a friend who met her husband—a crew member—on a cruise ship, and they are living happily ever after, some ten years later.

Another friend's daughter was romanced by a crew member who was only looking for an American to marry so he could have a "green card" and move to America. Never mind that he had—as was later discovered—a wife and four children in another country.

Consider it. Every week or so a new flock of ladies board a ship and the male crew, from the Captain on down, can look over the new buffet. One night at the Captain's table, I was teasing the Master of the vessel about, well, sex on board. He grinned and said, "Madame, when we are at sea we are all single." Go carefully, ladies.

To be perfectly fair, there are ships' officers who would never consider cheating on their wives. Tempting as those uniforms and practiced charm may be, I'll say it again. Go carefully, ladies.

I like to get an all-over tan. Are there places to take it all off on cruise ships?

Some ships allow topless sunbathing, almost always on the top deck. No children are allowed. Ask your travel agent for the ships which have this special feature. There are also chartered nude cruises where you don't have to wear anything. Before you ask, the crew and staff do *not* get down to the bare essentials. In researching a story about nude cruising, I learned that the greatest staff fear is on the part of the waiters. They are terrified of spilling hot soup on naked bazooms.

What do I do if my bags aren't in the baggage hall after I leave the ship?

Chances are about 99.99% that they *are* there, somewhere. Just go searching. This is a challenge if you have an "official" transfer from the pier to an airport because of the time pressure. The .01% is because someone else, feeling the same pressure, grabbed a bag that looked familiar. You can make a missing bag report at the pier—if you have time—or wait until you return home. Always make sure that essential return information is *inside* your bags.

How close can I cut a return flight to home?

How did you do in the casino? This is not the time to gamble. In the busiest ports, if your debarkation is at 9 a.m. anything before a 1 p.m. flight is frazzle-making. If your destination is a major city (think New York) a little more time would do wonders for your blood pressure. Sitting in an airport for an hour or two is lot less hassle-some than missing a flight and finding that the next one to your homeport on land is overbooked.

Chapter Twelve
Red Sails—and Eyes—in the Sunrise

Here comes the worst part . . . I didn't want to spoil your cruise through the pages of this book but, "Good Morning, America!" or whatever your final port may be.

The last night is when you wish the cruise could go on forever . . . particularly because there are a lot of nasty details demanding your attention. As if by magic, a number of small envelopes for tips appeared in your cabin in the afternoon—unless you are on the auto-tip method. They usually have cunning messages such as, "For My Cabin Steward." Your duty is clear. Stuff them with cash.

Sometime in the late afternoon a nice computer printout of everything you've charged to your sail and sign and sail card will also show up under your door, on the foot of your bed, or displayed on your desk. This is a "pre-bill," giving you the opportunity to dispute charges you think are incorrect. Give it a glance for glaring errors. This is not the moment to take spouse or offspring to task for what they did, indeed, spend. If you were charged for a shore excursion you didn't take, a sequined tuxedo rental or drinks in a bar on a night you were watching TV in the cabin, make a fuss. Now. If you don't, your final bill will be under the door in the morning, already charged to your credit card.

Many ships now offer the wonderful experience of watching your sail and spend card charges mount on the in-cabin TV.

Rats. Packing.

On your last night out, after enjoying the camaraderie of new friends for the last time, you must repack all those suitcases you so carefully packed a lifetime ago. And have them in the hall by, usually, 1:00 a.m.

Wise cruisers do the re-pack late in the afternoon, leaving only the last-minute carry-on for the morning. With luck, the packed bags will slide under the bed, out of the way. Otherwise, stack the packed bags tidily in a corner of your cabin to be put out later.

If you've been wise, along the way, you've *folded* most of those used clothes. They pack a lot better that way than in wads. And, when you pack, put the "cleans" on the bottom of suitcases and the "dirties" on top, separated by plastic bags. That way, when you get home you can ditch the stuff headed for the dry cleaner or washer almost immediately.

Some people choose to wear their next-day travel clothes to dinner. Others don't. Whichever your choice, don't forget you will *need* clothes tomorrow. There are plenty of sea-going legends about the folks who ever-so-carefully packed their last-night outfits and set the bags outside the door.

One friend, wearing only her robe and a smile, helped her husband—wearing only a pair of pajama pants—lug the suitcases into the hall. *Click!* The door was closed behind them and their key cards were in the cabin. It was quite late at night and *someone* got to go to the Purser's desk to request cabin re-entry.

There are too many stories to believe that they are apocryphal, of first-time cruisers—charmingly wrapped in sheets or bath towels—beseeching anyone who would listen that they really *needed* their bags back.

Even the most experienced cruisers can get nailed by the "last night stupids." Make sure, very sure, that everything you need for *tomorrow* is neatly laid out. That includes shoes.

⚠ Check to make sure that your cruise line baggage tags are *not* still attached to your luggage. If you leave the embarkation tags on, likely as not your luggage will be redelivered to your room the next day for the next cruise. This will be a surprise to your successors and a clear inconvenience for you.

With luck, all the luggage from a particular deck or the same disembarkation group ends up in the same area, making your collection process easier.

Of course, you won't empty your safe until the Last Morning and stow all the contents in the Giant Tote Bag.

It's a good idea to have some special identification method for your luggage, especially if it's black. A strip of colorful tape, a wildly-colored luggage strap or pompoms work well.

The Last Morning

On debarkation day, you may not be able to wake up and smell the coffee, as it probably won't be delivered by room service. And, after a week or more of living without a morning schedule, one is imposed—as in, out of your cabin by 8:00 a.m. Check the ship's newspaper to see where breakfast is being served. Sometimes the Main Dining Room doesn't offer a seated, order-from-the-menu breakfast and you're on your own to fight with everyone else at the buffet. There's a lot to be said for a bootlegged banana or apple on that last morning.

The most boresome activity as you wait—and wait and wait—at your arrival port is for the ship to be cleared and for passengers' shipboard accounts to be cleared. If you hear announcements asking for the same passengers' names over and over, it's for one of two reasons. First, a passenger's credit card company said, "No." Second, a foreign national didn't complete the proper Immigration paperwork.

The deadbeat will probably get off the ship. The foreign national will possibly be detained so you can get off.

The only weapons here are a good book, a bottle of water or can of soda, a piece of fruit and a cheery attitude. Don't murder your vacation with impatience and surliness at the end.

Boarding is usually a fairly leisurely process over a period of three or four hours. Fleeing the ship is much more intense. Debarkation cards with a number (or a letter, or a color) appear in your cabin on the night of The Last Supper. You'll be called to leave the ship in a pre-determined order, based on that card. People with fast flight connections usually receive preference, as do the handicapped and those in top cabins. How are the cruise lines clever enough to know all this? Passengers receive a debarkation form about mid-voyage which asks such essential information as flight times and numbers.

If you have been exceptionally nice (monetarily) to your cabin steward, you'll have no problem parking yourself in your cabin or on your balcony for as long as you wish—just so long he can do the requisite cleaning.

In the meantime, just before debarking, the public rooms are filled with huddled masses. Do your best to be cheerful. And don't jam the passageways. Take time to look around and wonder why all these people are so eager to get off the ship.

When do we clear Customs?

This is one of the most misunderstood terms in travel. The Customs people collect taxes on goods. That's why there is a Customs House or the equivalent in every port city. What you do clear is Immigration. It's complicated and that's why it's a smart idea to have a passport.

As examples, if the first U.S. port you come to on your return is the United States Virgin Islands, you will clear Immigration there. If you're sailing back into Miami or Ft. Lauderdale by way of Key West, have your passport ready in Key West, as it is the first United States landfall. You will be asked to show your passport or other identification before you may leave the ship. The ship's daily newspaper will tell you what to do.

Home Again, Home Again. . . . .

Regardless of how long it took to get there, your front door probably never looked so good. The mail can wait. The unpacking and laundry surely can wait. The dog can stay at the kennel for another day or the kids with Grandma. And you really don't need to eat *again*, do you?

Think about those clean sheets in the bedroom, reach into the fridge and haul out the bottle of Champagne and the wheel of good brie you stashed before departure, get the crackers from the pantry, put your feet up. Now's the time to start the first of a lifetime's reminisces. "And wasn't it fun when. . . ."

ABOUT THE AUTHOR

Pam Kane is a world-class author and traveler. She has visited over a hundred countries (and counting), six continents, all fifty states and flown over a million miles. *Happy Sails: The Carefree Cruiser's Handbook* is her twelfth book and her second about cruise travel. Her first, *Cruise Control*, was reliably the number one best-selling cruise travel book on Amazon.com.

She survived growing up as far from an ocean as any place could possibly be—Iowa. Carrying on deep, philosophical conversations with her father's dairy herd of Guernsey cows (all named for the wives of other local farmers) wasn't enough. As soon as she could, after the pesky college thing, she took to the air as a flight attendant with United Airlines for two years. She hasn't stayed home for too long since—except to raise four children. Ms. Kane says, "I will travel almost anywhere at the drop of a passport." And she does.

She lived in the Caribbean four years and brings a special insight to cruisers on those popular itineraries. She lived in both Italy and Luxembourg during her largely mis-spent youth and has traveled extensively "on the Continent," throughout the Antipodes and the Pacific Rim. Ms. Kane speaks two languages, English and Spanish—and can get along well enough to find the bathroom or order a beer in several others.

Ms. Kane is a member of the American Society of Journalists and Authors (ASJA), which has the highest admission standards in the world of writers. She is also a member of other travel-related writers' organizations including the North American Travel Journalists Association (NATJA).

Pam Kane has authored books about on-line communications and computer security, and is an internationally-known expert on the subject of computer viruses (*The Data Recovery Bible, Prodigy Made Easy, The Hitchhiker's Guide to the Electronic Highway* and several other titles). She has been a contributor to such magazines as *Home PC, Portable Computing* and *washingtonpost.com* (she was their "Dear Ms. Modem" columnist).

Ms. Kane has appeared on *Good Morning America, CNN, NBC News, CBS Evening News, Financial News Network, Late Night Philadelphia, Science Friday, The Osgood Chronicles* and *MSNBC.com* as the "HurriKANE Magnet." She is a regular contributor to *Cruise Travel* magazine, a former contributing editor of *Porthole Magazine*, was the "First Cruisers" editor for *cruisemates.com* and is an editor of *Travel World International*.

She lives near the Chesapeake Bay with her husband, who is sometimes called "Captain Queeg," their sailboat, *Off-Line*, four cats who don't go near the water, forty-seven koi and two goldfish who do.

If you have cruise questions for Pam Kane, please go to the website http://www.happysails.com and click on the e-mail form.

INDEX